COOKING WITH TRADER JOE'S

Cookbook

Lighten Up!

Susan Greeley, MS, RD

Photographs by Dan Komoda

Contents

Chapter 8 – Lean Lunching

Chapter 9 – Dinner's On

Contents

Thank-You Notes

This book is dedicated to my beautiful parents, Ann H. and F. Bart Cooper, who are now two angels, each sitting on one of my shoulders, guiding me. I couldn't have done it without them. I know how proud they are, and I owe it all to them.

Jürgen Meier — Thank you for coming into my life. Ti amo per sempre, mein Schatz.

Harrison, Benjamin, and Patrick — The apples of my eye and biggest blessings a mother could ever receive — thank you for choosing crazy me as your mommy! I hope someday you'll actually praise instead of complain about my cooking...

Anita Fresolone and Dan Komoda — Thank you both from the bottom of my heart, particularly for Dan's amazing photography skill, Anita's willingness to support me/us and sacrifice her husband for two months, and to both of you for many years of friendship and believing in LBR!

Claire Wyckoff receives my appreciation and gratitude for being such a tremendous asset guiding, proofreading and editing my work along my cookbook writing and publishing journey. Thanks for believing in a stranger you met on LinkedIn.

A big thank you goes to Heather World for the text trimming and awesome copy editing.

I'm extremely grateful to Deana Gunn and Wona Miniati for finding me and giving me this opportunity. Namaste!

Many, many thanks to my amazing, supportive friends, many of whom are happy recipe-testers. I'll keep cooking if you keep tasting and applauding! I love you all — don't make me name names. Just know I couldn't have done it without you!!

I have to give a big shout-out to all of my clients who inspire me and all those who honor me by listening and taking my advice. I will continue to do my best to help you live and feel better.

Thank God for the Internet, social networking, and most of all — Trader Joe's!

Introduction

D-I-E-T. This four-letter word conjures up thoughts of celery, cottage cheese, and rice cakes for every meal. Well, I suggest you ditch the curds and grab this book if you want to bring back the pleasure of eating while losing and maintaining a healthy weight. Eating healthy can be E-A-S-Y!

The good times start with Trader Joe's (TJ's), because it's a truly unique food store. You're happy the moment you enter and come face-to-face with fresh flowers and potted plants. TJ's wants you to relax: the employees are helpful and the coffee is free. TJ's makes your life easier: cheerful chalkboard signs advertise new foods and old favorites, and the sample bar offers up creative combinations of TJ greats. You'd think this cozy environment means high prices, but it doesn't. TJ's manages to offer a diverse selection of easily prepared foods at a low price. I love shopping there! My local TJ's displayed a photo of me holding my son in one arm and my favorite TJ's product in the other. (For the record, it's frozen Organic Brown Rice.) I take my clients shopping there. I meet my friends there. I have spontaneous recipe exchanges there. It is an integral part of my personal and professional lives.

As a nutritionist, I have recommended countless TJ foods to my clients. When I expanded my practice to include cooking demonstrations, I found myself using TJ's foods almost exclusively because they are fresh, inexpensive, and convenient.

This cookbook evolved out of my reliance on TJ practicality and my passion to help people reach a healthy weight without feeling deprived or stressed. Successful weight loss requires commitment. Why **Lighten Up**? Because you can commit to my menu of easy, inexpensive, and practical recipes. You can commit to the long-term diet changes for maintaining healthy weight when you see short-term results. Finally, you can commit to starting it all with a great shopping experience. Lighten Up and have F-U-N!

Chapter 1

About Susan

My Nutrition Mission

I chose a health profession for a reason: I'm on a nutrition mission to change the way America eats, one person at a time, while maintaining fun, freedom, and flavor.

The things we eat are undeniably linked to our health, happiness, and overall well-being. Yet somehow, most of us still don't get it right.

Successful weight management isn't about eliminating all fats or carbs. It's not about cabbage soup or grapefruit for days at a time. Successful weight management boils down to making good food choices and staying active. It's that simple.

However, simple doesn't necessarily mean obvious. That's where I help my clients and where I can help you. I teach people how to make the right diet choices daily and to give them the tools they need to lose weight, or simply maintain a healthy weight and feel great. I make lots of simple yet effective diet recommendations, and I see the positive results every day.

My Food Foundation

What we eat in childhood sets the foundation for our health for the rest of our lives. I consider myself pretty darn lucky because I had a smart start, thanks to my parents. Money was tight in our household of 10. (Yes, I had seven siblings!) My health and budget-conscious father never bought junk food except as an occasional treat. Packaged cookies, processed sweets and potato chips made it into our home about once a year. My father also preached moderation in all things.

While conservative in many regards, my parents were liberal about exposure to foreign cultures. My father's work took him overseas, and when my parents eventually moved back to small-town Ohio, my mother regaled us with food adventures from around the world: sampling *schwarzwurzel,* a root vegetable from Switzerland, dining on the stewed meat and beans the Brazilians call *feijoada,* or diving into a plate of eggplant Parmesan from Italy. Our meals included exotic foods bought on special shopping trips to Cleveland and Pittsburgh.

Thanks to Mom, I know that if you expand your culinary world, you'll see a wide variety of healthy, delicious food. I can turn a can of pumpkin purée into a soup, a pasta, a dessert, a muffin or bread, and I know that beans and greens aren't just peasant food. I'm thankful for my food foundation. It wasn't always gourmet, but it was always healthful and homemade.

My Profession: Food & Nutrition Expert

Infected by my parents' enthusiasm for travel, I spent my senior year of high school in Germany. I quickly learned that this is a country of no-nonsense eating. Germany is known for its *vollkornbrot*, a dense whole-grain rye bread popularly served at breakfast. Germans build festivals around the seasonal appearance of vegetables like white asparagus and chanterelle mushrooms. Here I found a wide array of cookbooks focused on whole-grain cooking.

In college, I studied Chemistry and German, but I gravitated toward nutrition and wound up with a degree in Dietetics. I moved to Boston to complete training as a dietitian. I earned a Master of Science in Nutrition Communication from Tufts University when the field was relatively unknown.

Now, 17 years since I became a Registered Dietitian, the need for nutrition communicators seems to be growing in tandem with our national waistline. For the past five years, I've been a nutrition consultant, counselor, speaker, and writer helping others achieve their personal weight and health goals. I write and cook recipes all the time, and I love Trader Joe's, so let's get started!

Chapter 2

Lighten Up for Life: A Daily Diet To End Dieting

Curb Cravings with Good Carbs and Lose Abdominal Fat

The best way to fight fat and ditch diets is to eat most of your daily calories from carbohydrates. This is not a fad; it's science. However, not all carbohydrates are created equal. When you understand the difference between good carbs and bad carbs, you're on your way to winning the weight battle for life.

Good Carbs Unveiled

When you eat good carbs, you're filling yourself with fiber, phytochemicals, and (good) fats that are vital to your health. What does this mean for you?

> **Good carbs reduce the cravings that trigger poor food choices and overeating**

- Good carbs give you energy. The body needs fuel, and carbohydrates are the right level of octane.

- Good carbs help you lose that muffin top and jelly belly. Studies show it, but the real proof is in doing it. If you snack on pretzels now, change them to edamame or fruit or hummus and vegetables. That's an easy start, and you will see a difference in your waistline.

- Good carbs reduce cravings that trigger poor food choices and overeating. Eat good carbs and your cravings will subside as your body is filled with much-needed fiber, phytochemicals, and good fats.

- Many good carbs keep us hydrated. Most fruits and vegetables in particular have a high water content. Water, in turn, fills our stomachs and keeps us from overeating. It also helps us feel more energetic and keeps everything in our intestinal tract moving along (and out)!

- Good carbs maintain a healthy acid-base balance in the body. The body likes to be more alkaline, and many of the foods we eat (high protein diets, refined carbs, caffeine) create a more acidic environment that leaves us prone to disease. Most fruits and vegetables and some grains, legumes, and nuts counteract that.

- Good carbs prevent chronic disease. How many times have we all heard that fruits and vegetables help ward off disease? Apparently not enough, if our country's weight problems are the gauge!

Good carbs help you lose that muffin top and jelly belly

So which carbs are good? It's a short general list, but the overall number and variety of foods in these food groups is extensive enough to offer even picky palates enough great foods.

- **Fruits.** There are no bad fruits. Most Americans eat far too few. (Avocados are the one fruit whose calories come primarily from fat and not carbohydrates. It is known as a "superfood" and should be part of the diet to provide good fats, but it is higher in calories than other fruits and should not be eaten freely.)

- **Vegetables.** There are no bad vegetables, either. Eat more, eat many!

- **Whole Grains.** The key word here is "whole," because anything else is refined and not healthful. Consuming more whole grains provides vital micronutrients and fiber that many people are lacking. These grains also provide protein and small amounts of essential fats. And there are so many! Keep things interesting by going beyond brown rice and experiment with quinoa, millet, whole wheatberries, oats, barley, and amaranth.

- **Legumes.** Also known as beans but not limited to beans, these little gems offer the best source of fiber in the diet and complex carbohydrates as well as protein. Many Americans eat few to no legumes but should be incorporating them into daily meals. Why? Because the more fiber you eat, the more pounds you'll shed in the long run. Whether canned, dried, or fresh, legumes added to your daily –or at least weekly – diet is beneficial, cheap and easy. Some of my top recommendations are edamame (young soy beans), lentils, black beans, chickpeas, cannellini beans (white kidney or great northern), fava beans, kidney beans, lima beans, black-eyed peas. If you encounter any other others you like, eat them!

The more fiber you eat, the more pounds you'll shed in the long run

Bad Carbs Exposed

While I like to focus on the positives, I can't overlook the need to identify the opposite of good carbs. Know your enemy! Generally speaking, bad carbs are found in sugars and refined foods.

Bad Carb Foods

- **All refined sugars and sweeteners.** Table sugar, brown sugar, evaporated cane sugar, honey, agave syrup, maple syrup, high-fructose corn syrup are the best known. Other less known sweeteners are sugar alcohols, including sorbitol, xylitol and mannitol, and the now popular plant sweetener stevia. Some are touted as healthful, but the bottom line is that all are refined sugars and sweeteners that should be limited in the diet.

- **Alcohol.** Drinking red wine in moderation has its health benefits, but don't forget that alcohol is a sugar, which puts it into the "bad carb" category.

- **White flour.** Don't be confused by the labels. "Wheat flour," "enriched wheat flour" and "unbleached wheat flour" sound wholesome but are not. Bleached or unbleached, unless it says "whole wheat," there's nothing whole about it.

> **Know your bad carbs: avoid sugars and refined grains, flours and other highly processed foods**

Food manufacturers work hard to convince us we're eating right when really we're eating wrong. Here is a list of seemingly good-for-you foods that are loaded with "bad" refined carbs:

White flour pastas, white refined rices, pretzels, fat-free cookies, breakfast bars, fat-free yogurts and salad dressings, regular and baked or fat-free chips.

Bad Carb Blues

What's the big deal with flour and sugar? If my cookies are homemade, aren't they an acceptable snack? Unfortunately, processed and refined foods:

- Wreak havoc on blood sugar, energy levels and hormones.
- Cause inflammation in the body, which contributes to obesity and fuels most chronic disease.
- Leave us unsatisfied and trigger cravings for sugar.
- Serve as the strongest "trigger foods" for stress eaters and food addicts.
- Exacerbate stress levels.

> **Bad carbs leave us unsatisfied and trigger cravings for sugar**

While we don't have to remove these carbs indefinitely from our diet, it does help to "detox" from them occasionally and get to a point where they are eaten infrequently and not multiple times a day or in excessive quantities.

*Eliminating **bad** carbs is not the same as eliminating **all** carbs. That is the difference between a fad diet and the Lighten Up for Life diet.*

Fad Diets or Fat Diets?
How Dieting Has Made Americans Fat

Over the past two decades, Americans have fallen prey to two particular diet trends that have fattened our population. The false promise behind both is the same: eat as much as you want, just don't eat certain things.

Fat-Free Fiasco

In the 1990's, "fat" became an evil word, and just about every food manufacturer scrambled to develop tasty foods with little or no fat of any kind. Unfortunately, the science behind the fat fear was over-simplified and misinterpreted; the message that we need good fats for health and vitality went missing in the media.

Normal portions and common sense fell by the wayside as dieters gobbled up entire boxes of fat-free cookies and packages of snack foods in one sitting. In this world, a fat-free muffin the size of your fist was a better food than an avocado. Not surprisingly, Americans grew bigger, and the incidence of heart disease and diabetes soared. The mistake was identified, but the backlash diet that followed was equally harmful.

High-Protein, No-Carb Confusion

Starting in the next decade, "carbs" became the evil word. Protein was the new solution. Dieters ditched bananas and dove into chicken and cheese. This fad was even more insidious than the fat-free craze, because a low-calorie, high-protein diet will result in early weight loss. The success caught on like wildfire, and just about every restaurant and food manufacturer jumped on board once again.

Unfortunately, weight loss from a high protein diet is unsustainable. Dieters regained weight — often more than they initially lost — when they resumed "normal" eating. Weight wasn't the only thing gained. So were an increased incidence of colon cancer, hypertension, kidney disease, osteoporosis, diabetes, and heart disease.

Weight loss from a high protein diet is unsustainable

The Demise of Diet Myths and Delusions

Frustrated dieters were left confused. I want to dispel these myths so that you can make good food choices for yourself.

Myth: Fat makes you fat.

Truth: Getting enough good fat in your diet will help you lose weight and stay healthy.

Myth: Carbs are bad.

Truth: Not all carbohydrates are created equally. Most of your calories should come from "good" carbohydrates. Eating whole grains and legumes in particular really will help you reduce abdominal fat.

Myth: A high protein diet is the way to lose weight.

Truth: Not at the expense of good carbs and fats. High protein diets typically add saturated fat and sodium and decrease fiber, water, and micronutrients. They are low in calories and high in deprivation.

Myth: Cutting calories makes you lose weight.

Truth: In the most technical sense, this may be true, but I don't see that in practice. Calorie-restrictive diets lower your resting metabolic rate and set you up for a lifetime of weight-cycling, which leads to altered body composition (less lean body mass and more fat mass).

Myth: Deprivation is part of dieting.

Truth: NO diet will work long-term if you constantly feel deprived.

Delusion: "I know what I *should* be eating."

Reality: You truly believe you do, but in my experience, you don't. My clients are usually surprised by the wide variety of foods they can eat.

Delusion: "I usually eat healthy foods!"

Reality: Most people aren't aware of what they eat every day until they track it.

Delusion: "I'm middle-aged now and have no metabolism! Everything I eat goes straight to my _____ (pick a body part)."

Reality: Over the course of years, we develop habits that slow our metabolisms, such as skipping meals and consuming toxins in foods without knowing it. Age does play a role — after 35, our resting metabolic rate decreases — but the decrease is slight. It's not the problem. Despite advertising claims to the contrary, the miracle "metabolism boost" is a diet of whole foods that is high in natural fiber, good fat, and phytochemicals. This cleaner diet helps to cleanse the liver, which in turn improves metabolism.

> The miracle metabolism boost is from a diet high in fiber, good fats, and phytochemicals – i.e., good carbs!

5 Daily Diet Rules

These are my simple rules for maintaining a healthy weight:

1. **Eat most of your daily calories from good carbs (fruits, vegetables, whole grains, and legumes).**

2. **Minimize bad carbs (refined sugars, alcohol, and white flour products).**

3. **Drink 8 ounces water 15-30 minutes before meals.**

4. **Sit down and chew longer instead of standing or eating on-the-go.**

5. **Count calories only for calorie-dense foods such as oils, nuts, and fruits like avocado (see chart on p. 24).**

5 Suggested Weight-Loss Tools

1. Keep a food diary. In the beginning, track what you eat, whether on an electronic device or hand-written notebook. It's best to capture all the details: the food or drink, the amount, the time.

2. Increase daily physical activity. Add 15 minutes of walking a day, and you add years to your life. Every minute of sedentary time turned into active time burns calories and improves health.

3. Find a non-food related stress-relieving activity. Food is a great comfort, so finding a replacement is critically important. Try yoga, blast the stereo and dance, walk the dog, paint, read a magazine, do the crossword puzzle, call a friend. Choose something that alleviates stress rather than pushes it off the way food and drink (i.e., alcohol) do.

4. Seek positive support. Support — from a dietitian, a partner, a work colleague, a friend — is a key factor in losing and maintaining weight.

5. Use this cookbook!

Chapter 3

2-Week Weight Loss Challenge:
The jump-start diet that will change your life

Who Needs It
The 2-week diet challenge may be for you if you...

- really want to lose weight and need a jump-start.
- have been a yo-yo dieter for years.
- are frustrated because you've reached a plateau and can't get past it.
- are healthy, health-conscious and simply looking to "eat better" or "detox" from refined foods and feel better.

The benefits depend on your commitment to the full two weeks. You've got nothing to lose — except unwanted pounds — and much to gain. I don't advise procrastination, but timing does matter. Please don't start this diet right before a two-week string of planned parties, special events, or dinners out.

After the 2-Week Challenge, re-read chapter two of this book to drive home daily diet habits that will keep you lightened up for life.

What Not To Eat
For two weeks, all of the following are to be removed from your diet:

- All refined flours and sugars. NO sugars, syrups, jellies, honey, agave syrup or other forms of sugar. NO white flour or other refined flours, including pasta.
- Cheese and nearly all dairy. (Milk in coffee or tea is the exception.)
- Processed potatoes, including chips and fries. (Baked, roasted, or boiled potatoes are allowed.)
- Alcohol.
- Sweetened beverages.
- Artificial sweeteners.
- Preservatives and flavor enhancers such as monosodium glutamate (MSG).

What To Eat

Your daily diet for the two weeks will include a lot of fresh foods. You may have to shop more than one time per week, but keeping the foods on hand is imperative to the 2-Week Challenge success. Think "3 P's": planning, purchasing, preparing.

Foods to include daily:

- Fresh fruits (no dried fruits). Eat as many as you want.
- Vegetables, salads. Eat at least one large salad, preferably with dinner, to fill up and not overeat other, heavier foods.
- Whole grains, including sprouted grain bread, brown rice, quinoa, oats, barley and any others you like.
- One ounce of nuts or seeds (about a fistful), including nut butters.
- Legumes. You have a wide range of options here, including beans, peas and edamame.
- Lean meats, fish, poultry and eggs. Grass-fed beef and organic, free-range meats and eggs recommended.
- Good fats from nuts, seeds, olive oil, avocado, fish, eggs, and grass-fed beef.

Sample Menu for 2-Week Challenge

This one-week menu removes the thinking and decision-making related to food preparation. I recommend automating breakfast and snacks, and adding more variety with lunches and dinner.

Before you begin, there are a few things to point out about the diet and recipes.

1. There are foods known to specifically cleanse the liver and potentially boost your metabolism. They are included in many of the recipes in this book and should be eaten frequently:

- Eggs
- Mushrooms
- Parsley
- Lemons
- Beets
- Artichokes
- Root vegetables

Egg yolks contain choline and lecithin in addition to all amino acids, omega 3's and vitamins. Choline is an essential part of phospholipids that helps us regulate cholesterol and fat (and prevent both from accumulating in the liver). It is a building block for cell membranes and is essential for brain and cardiovascular health. Lecithin is an emulsifier and main component of bile.

2. While I do preach eating "as much as you want" of low-calorie, high-water content fruits and vegetables and *not* counting calories, this is not a free pass to throw portion control out the window for *all* foods. Limiting calorie-dense foods is a must. Limit the challenge's calorie-dense foods: olive oil, nuts, nut butters, avocados, potatoes, and portions of meats. After the challenge, if and when you reintroduce dairy, measure and limit cheese, cream cheese, sour cream, milk, and cream.

3. Coffee and teas are both permitted. Both have health-promoting phytochemicals and are not detrimental to your diet. The challenge comes only if you typically take sugar or sweetener in either. *No sweeteners (sugar or artificial), non-dairy creamers or other creamers with hydrogenated oils* can be used. A small amount of milk (cow, soy, or other) is permitted in coffee or tea.

4. Throughout the cookbook, recipes that are appropriate for the 2-Week Challenge are marked with the icon:

	Breakfast	Lunch	Dinner	Snacks/Dessert
Day 1	1 cup cooked oatmeal, prepared with apples, 1 tsp. ground flax, dash of cinnamon Coffee or tea	Sandwich Love (p. 108)	Try It You'll Like It Turkey Chili (p. 58) Brown rice Standby Green Salad (p. 74)	Apple 1 oz almonds per day More fruit as desired (berries, melon, other)
Day 2	2 slices Ezekiel bread 2 tsp Earth Balance 2 fried eggs ½ cup orange juice or fresh fruit Coffee or tea	Turkey chili (leftover)	Chicken Balsamico (p. 122) Asparagus Brown Rice Red & Green Salad (p. 81)	Apple 1 oz almonds per day More fruit as desired
Day 3	Healthy Huevos (p. 36) ½ cup orange juice or fresh fruit Coffee or tea	Sandwich Love (p. 108) Double Bean & Basil Salad (p. 92)	Skillet Shrimp & Quinoa (p. 145) Standby Green Salad (p. 74)	Apple 1 oz almonds per day More fruit as desired
Day 4	2 slices Ezekiel bread, toasted 1 Tbsp almond butter 1 banana (or other fruit) Coffee or tea	Asian Chopped Chicken Salad (p. 103)	Dijon Salmon w/ Artichokes (p. 140) Loaded Black Bean Salad (p. 100)	Apple More fruit as desired
Day 5	1 cup cooked oatmeal, prepared with apples, 1 tsp. ground flax, dash of cinnamon Coffee or tea	Egg Salad Sandwich (p. 111) Light & Lemony Lentils (p. 170)	Spicy Quinoa, Black Bean & Mushroom Soup (p. 60) Standby Green Salad (p. 74)	Apple 1 oz almonds per day More fruit as desired
Day 6	2 slices Ezekiel bread, toasted 1 Tbsp. almond butter 1 banana (or other fruit) Coffee or tea	Spicy Quinoa, Black Bean & Mushroom Soup (leftover)	Roast Rosemary Pork (p. 139) Light & Lemony Lentils (leftover) Cumin Carrots (p. 176) Standby Green Salad (p. 74)	Apple 1 oz almonds per day More fruit as desired
Day 7	1 cup cooked oatmeal, prepared with chopped apple, 1 tsp. ground flax, dash of cinnamon Coffee or tea	Move Over Cobb, It's Melt In Your Mouth Mâche (p. 91)	Asian-Style Beef with Cabbage & Mushrooms (p. 135) Brown Rice Standby Green Salad (p. 74)	Apple More fruit as desired

Calorie-Dense Foods to Measure & Limit

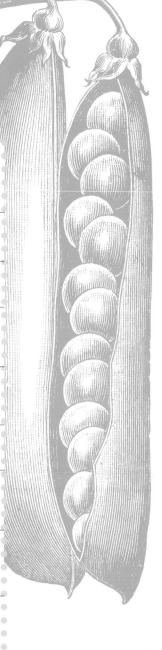

Food Group	Foods
Fats/Oils	All oils and solid fats (butter, margarine)
Meats	Red meats, processed meats including cold cuts, sausage, bacon, fried chicken and fish
Dairy	All cheeses and creams, sour cream, whole milk dairy products
Nuts	All nuts and nut butters
Fruits	Avocados, dried fruits
Vegetables	Mashed potatoes, any fried vegetables (including chips and French fries)
Condiments, Sauces, Soups	Mayonnaise, cream sauces, gravies, creamy soups, etc.
Sweets & Alcohol	Wine, beer, hard alcohol & liqueurs Ice cream, cakes, brownies, pies, etc.

About the Recipes

Each recipe in this book contains ingredients that can be found at Trader Joe's. While many of the ingredients are generic, ingredients that are capitalized are specific products found at Trader Joe's.

Each recipe indicates the total time, which includes prep time and cooking time.

Each recipe contains nutritional data. Optional ingredients are not included when calculating nutritional data. Serving sizes follow FDA guidelines and my recommendations.

Each recipe contains indicators for recipes that are

gluten-free   **vegetarian**   **2-Week Challenge**

Please note that the FDA has not established a standard to define the term gluten-free. Products at Trader Joe's may be labeled "no gluten ingredients used" which does not necessarily exclude the chance of cross-contamination if it is produced in a facility that handles gluten products. Persons with celiac disease or severe gluten allergies should note that unless a product is labeled and tested gluten-free by standards such as ELISA and produced in a dedicated facility, there is possibility of cross-contamination.

Starting the day off with good nutrition is key to long-term weight management and overall health. Many people skip the "most important meal of the day," and that works against their metabolism. Your car won't start without gas, and your body doesn't like it either! Many of us have little time, but there are quick and easy ways to get a nutritious breakfast to fuel your body. In addition to the recommended 2-Week Challenge breakfast ideas, this chapter gives delicious options for making the most of breakfast. Focus on getting a combination of good carbs with fiber, protein, and little or no added sugar to help keep your blood sugar even throughout the morning. If breakfast really is not your thing, fruit is the best fuel to grab, or make a smoothie to go.

The bottom line:
Take time to start
the day off right!

Chapter 4

Rethinking Breakfast

Pan-Fried Polenta with Warm Blueberries

Polenta is a quick, delicious, low-calorie and often over-looked breakfast food. Polenta, or cornmeal mush as my Kentucky-born mother called it, is a satisfying way to start your day, and the sunny color will brighten your morning!

Single serving
Total time 10 minutes

 **Omit agave syrup**

4 slices precooked Organic Polenta, ¼ inch thick
½ Tbsp unsalted butter or Earth's Balance
½ cup frozen blueberries
1 Tbsp agave syrup *(omit during 2-Week Challenge)*
1 lemon

1 Rinse berries to thaw slightly and pour into a glass measuring cup. Add agave syrup and microwave on high for 1 minute.

2 In a medium-sized cast-iron skillet or frying pan, heat butter over medium heat just until it begins to bubble. Add polenta slices and lightly fry on each side until golden brown, about 3 or 4 minutes per side.

3 Place polenta on serving plate and pour berries on top. Add lemon zest as desired.

Nutrition Snapshot
Per serving: 230 calories, 6.5g fat, 3.5g saturated fat, 2g protein, 42g carbs, 4g fiber, 310mg sodium

 Gluten Free   Vegetarian

Better Than PB&J Wrap

If you're a fan of peanut butter and banana, you're going to fall in love with this wrap. I did! It makes a delicious meal for breakfast or lunch. You can also eat half now and save half for a snack any time of day — either way, it's a healthy, portable breakfast wrap.

Single serving
Total time 3 minutes

1 Whole Grain Flour Tortilla with rolled oats and flax seeds

1 ½ Tbsp sunflower butter

½ banana

1 tsp honey

1 Tbsp sliced almonds

Dash cinnamon

1 Spread sunflower butter on tortilla.

2 Slice banana and layer on top of sunflower butter, then drizzle with honey and almonds.

3 Sprinkle with cinnamon as desired, fold and eat.

Nutrition Snapshot
Per wrap: 400 calories, 19g fat, 2g saturated fat, 12g protein, 50g carbs, 11g fiber, 230mg sodium

 **G** Gluten Free Use brown rice tortilla

Breakfast Spinach-Egg Wrap

Eggs are a real fast food, so if breakfast has to be quick, you can whip this up in just a couple of minutes, wrap it, and go. For getting more family members fed and out the door, this recipe can easily be doubled or quadrupled!

Single serving
Total time 8 minutes

1 Whole Grain Flour Tortilla with rolled oats and flax seeds

Olive oil or canola spray

2 eggs

1 cup fresh spinach

1 oz grated Lite Celtic Cheddar

Salt and pepper to taste

1   Whisk eggs with 1 Tbsp water in a small bowl and set aside.

2   Spray small frying pan with olive oil or canola spray and heat on medium heat. Add tortilla, heat about one minute just to brown slightly, and crisp one side. Transfer to plate.

3   Add spinach to pan and cook until it wilts, stirring with a wooden spatula.

4   Pour eggs on top of spinach and cook and stir, until eggs are fully cooked.

5   Place egg scramble in center of tortilla. Sprinkle with grated cheese, and season with salt and pepper.

6   Fold sides of tortilla over eggs to form a wrap.

Nutrition Snapshot
Per wrap: 350 calories, 16g fat, 6g saturated fat, 25g protein, 26g carbs, 6g fiber, 515mg sodium

 **Use brown rice tortilla**

Sweet Onion and Broccoli Frittata

A frittata is an Italian version of an omelet and an example of how simple, fresh, and healthful the Italians make their food. A frittata is a go-to, nutritious, and delicious meal that requires virtually no prep. TJ's Frozen Balsamic Glazed Grilled Sweet Onions — imported from Italy — just begged me to put them into this frittata! They are simply delicious and give it a gourmet touch with no effort. Onions may not seem like nutritional powerhouses, but they are loaded with disease-fighting phytochemicals. Make your own variation by adding fresh herbs or other vegetables such as asparagus, zucchini, or bell peppers.

6 **Servings**
Total time 20 minutes

Omit Parmesan cheese

6 eggs
½ (12-oz) pkg or 2 cups broccoli florets
½ (10-oz) pkg Frozen Balsamic Glazed Grilled Sweet Onions
¼ tsp salt
⅛ tsp pepper
¼ cup water
2 Tbsp shredded Parmesan cheese *(omit during 2-Week Challenge)*
Olive oil cooking spray

1 In a small frying pan, heat sweet onions over medium heat. Let cook 3 minutes, breaking apart frozen onions and letting them thaw and soften.

2 Add broccoli and cook with onions another 3-4 minutes.

3 In a glass bowl, whisk together eggs with salt, pepper and water.

4 Heat a 9-inch iron omelet pan and spray with cooking spray oil.

5 Add broccoli and onions to eggs and pour into warmed pan.

6 Let frittata cook over medium-low heat until eggs set.

7 Sprinkle with Parmesan cheese and put in oven on broil for about one minute to fully cook eggs and slightly brown cheese.

Note *Serve immediately or make ahead and refrigerate for lunch or dinner. Serve with arugula, mâche, or other salad.*

Nutrition Snapshot
Per ¹/₆ th frittata: 112 calories, 7g fat, 2g saturated fat, 8g protein, 4g carbs, 0.5g fiber, 260mg sodium

Healthy Huevos

Huevos rancheros is a delicious brunch food that is typically laden with too much fat, sodium, and more calories than you might want or need for breakfast or brunch. Replacing the tortillas with brown rice and eliminating beans and cheese that have been added to many versions translates into a quick, easy "power breakfast" and tasty way to have your huevos any day of the week. Bacon lovers, this one's for you! (Moderation is key.)

Single serving
Total time 5-10 minutes

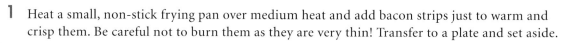

1 cup (½ pouch) frozen Organic Brown Rice

1 egg

Olive oil or canola spray

¼ cup Smoky Peach Salsa *(substitute another salsa during 2-Week Challenge)*

3 strips Fully Cooked Uncured Bacon

Peach salsa contains added sugar. Substitute any salsa with no added sugar

1   Heat a small, non-stick frying pan over medium heat and add bacon strips just to warm and crisp them. Be careful not to burn them as they are very thin! Transfer to a plate and set aside.

2   Microwave brown rice according to instructions (3 minutes) and place on plate.

3   Wipe pan clean and spray with cooking spray. Fry egg over medium heat, until yolk is firm, or to your liking.

4   Place egg on rice and top with salsa. Add dash of salt and pepper if desired. Serve with bacon on the side.

Note   for non-meat eaters, leave off the bacon and add another egg. This variation also reduces the sodium by two thirds!

Nutrition Snapshot
Per serving: 360 calories, 13g fat, 4g saturated fat, 17g protein, 42g carbs, 2.5g fiber, 720mg sodium

 **Omit bacon**

Great Griddle Cakes

Waking up to pancakes and coffee can start your day with a smile, but many people have put pancakes on the no-no list. When you give traditional American pancakes a multigrain makeover, they're no longer a forbidden food. Just be mindful of how much butter and syrup go on top! I typically make these with the apple-banana combination, but peach-banana is a delicious variation.

6 **Servings** (makes 12 pancakes)
Total time 15 minutes

1 ¾ cups Multigrain Baking and Pancake Mix
1 cup old-fashioned rolled oats (not instant or steel-cut)
2 cups Unsweetened Soy Milk or organic skim milk
1 very ripe banana, mashed
1 egg
1 apple, peeled and chopped
¼ tsp cinnamon
Canola spray
1 tsp butter per serving (optional)
1 Tbsp agave syrup per serving (optional)

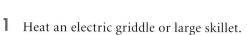

1 Heat an electric griddle or large skillet.

2 Add pancake mix and oats to a mixing bowl. Pour in milk and stir well.

3 Add mashed banana, egg, apple, and cinnamon; stir just until combined.

4 Spray griddle with canola spray. Pour ¼ cup of batter per pancake, cook until bubbly on top, then flip and cook another 1 minute.

5 Serve immediately with a teaspoon of butter and a drizzle of Organic Raw Blue Agave Sweetener per serving.

Note *One Tbsp agave syrup adds 60 calories. One tsp butter adds 30 calories.*

Nutrition Snapshot

2 pancakes per serving: 315 calories, 6.5g fat, 1g saturated fat,
13g protein, 52g carbs, 6.5g fiber, 450mg sodium

Swiss-Style Muesli

When I was an exchange student in Germany, my host mother would serve homemade muesli for breakfast almost daily. She would soak old-fashioned oats in milk all night and then mix them with a variety of fresh fruit, nuts, yogurt, and honey in the morning. Years later, I do the same thing because I find it healthier and better than granola and not quite as boring as a regular bowl of oatmeal. This is my favorite version, but you can of course make your own mix of fruit, such as oranges, banana or berries, or dried fruit and nuts, but be aware that both dried fruits and nuts increase the calories quite a bit. It can be made in the morning – oats need an hour to soak – or at night to let the oats soak overnight.

4 **Servings**
Total time 8-10 minutes after soaking oats

1 cup old-fashioned rolled oats

3 Tbsp ground flax seed

1 cup unsweetened soy milk (or other milk of choice)

1 large apple

½ cup sliced seedless red grapes

1 ½ cups plain organic nonfat yogurt (or nonfat Greek yogurt)

1 Tbsp honey

¼ tsp cinnamon

2 Tbsp sliced almonds (optional)

1 Combine oats, flax and soy milk in a medium-sized bowl. Cover and refrigerate for 1 hour or overnight.

2 Peel and then grate apple into oat mixture.

3 Add grapes, then stir in yogurt.

4 Drizzle honey on top, sprinkle with cinnamon and almonds to serve.

Nutrition Snapshot
Per 1-cup serving: 310 calories, 6g fat, 0.5g saturated fat,
16g protein, 50g carbs, 8g fiber, 75mg sodium

  Use oats tested for gluten

Smart Start Breakfast Smoothie

If you prefer to drink your breakfast — at home or on-the-go — this one gives you all you need to get you going with plenty of vitamin C, calcium, potassium, protein and some good carbs to start the day. This smoothie is perfect post-workout too, so take it to the gym if you're a morning exerciser who doesn't like to eat beforehand. Frozen bananas are a good habit for smoothie drinkers — they add fiber, potassium, good carbs, and thickness to any smoothie.

Single serving
Total time 3-5 minutes

- ¾ cup orange juice with calcium
- ¾ cup organic nonfat yogurt
- 1 frozen banana
- 2 tsp flax with blueberries
- 1 tsp sugar (optional)

1 Blend all ingredients in a blender until smooth. Pour into a drinking glass or travel thermos. Drink immediately.

Note *Add 1-2 ice cubes if taking it to go.*

Nutrition Snapshot
Per serving: 310 calories, 2g fat, 0g saturated fat, 14g protein, 62g carbs, 4.5g fiber, 140mg sodium

Vegetarian   Gluten Free

Add nutrition to your diet with snacks that also help you lose weight. Unlimited grazing can add pounds, but the right snack foods in the right amounts become powerful little meals that fuel your body properly and prevent cravings. Many people think of a snack as something straight out of a package. This chapter has a list of better choices, including packaged snack foods found at TJ's as well as easy recipes. In general, a snack is simply a smaller meal, and just about any food can fit if not overdone on the portion. During the 2-Week Challenge, the snacking focus is on raw foods, good fats, and fiber. Fruit can be eaten any time and basically in any amount — by the time you've pigged out on fruit, there's no room for anything else! Higher calorie foods such as nuts and guacamole must be measured. When it comes to high-water-content, low-calorie fruits and vegetables, portion control is *not* encouraged.

Chapter 5

Smart
Snacks
and
Smoothies

Anytime and  "Free" Snacks

These snacks can fill you up, reduce cravings, and get you in the habit of snacking on low-calorie fruits and veggies. When you just need to munch, that's where popcorn comes in!

- Papaya with fresh lemon juice and mint
- Watermelon
- Simply fruit salad
- Grape tomatoes, celery, baby carrots mix with 2 Tbsp guacamole or hummus
- ½ cup shelled edamame
- 3 cups popcorn

2-Week Challenge 200-calorie Snacks

- 1 organic apple plus 15 almonds
- 4 pieces Brown Rice Sushi
- "Better than PB &J Bagel" (½ whole wheat bagel with almond butter, blackberries and cinnamon)
- 3 Tbsp Avocado's Number Guacamole (or homemade) plus 8 Reduced Guilt Woven Wheats Wafers (or Triscuits)
- 3 Tbsp Hummus (any) plus 10 multigrain tortilla chips, such as Veggie and Flaxseed Tortilla Chips
- 4 Tbsp Hummus or guacamole with 4 Woven Wheats Wafers plus carrots, celery, grape tomatoes, and/or cucumbers
- No-sugar-added, whole grain "allowed" crackers and chips:
    Woven Wheats Wafers
    Veggie and Flaxseed Tortilla Chips
    Multigrain Tortilla Chips
- 100-calorie spreads/dips:
    4 Tbsp Avocado's Number Guacamole
    4 Tbsp original hummus
    1 Tbsp peanut butter or almond butter (or other nut butters)
- Salsa is a "free" dip — just measure portion of chips if using them to dip.

Except Woven Wheats, mini bagel & baguette, ak-mak® crackers -- can substitute with rice crackers and rice cakes

Post-Challenge Under 300-Calorie Snacks

These snacks can double as breakfast!

- ½ cup seedless red grapes and 1 whole wheat mini-bagel or ½ whole bagel with:
    1 Tbsp peanut butter or nut butter,
    1 Light Creamy Swiss or Garlic and Herb Laughing Cow,
    or 2 Tbsp hummus
- 1 cup vanilla or plain yogurt with pomegranate seeds, flax, and cinnamon
- 1 cup Greek yogurt with apple, flax, 1 tsp honey, and cinnamon
- 1 cup Greek yogurt with berries and 1 tsp agave syrup
- ¼ cup nuts or trail mix — any variety
- 1 KIND Plus Bar (cranberry almond + antioxidants)
- 5 ak-mak® sesame crackers (110 calories) with 1 ½ Tbsp nut butter or ¼ cup hummus or guacamole
- 1 frozen Mini Baguette heated with 1 oz fresh goat or mozzarella cheese, tomato, and basil (mini pizza)
- Smoothies — refer to the following pages

Vegetarian **G** Gluten Free

Except Woven Wheats, mini bagel & baguette, ak-mak® crackers -- can substitute with rice crackers and rice cakes

Smoothies

Some words just make us feel better. I think "milkshake" is one of them! Kids and adults alike love a good old-fashioned milkshake, but with as many as 2,000 calories and 130 grams of (unhealthy) fat, it really does belong on the once-in-a-blue-moon list. However, there are ways to enjoy your shake without adding more than two days' worth of sugar and saturated fat. Smoothies can be made from any variety of fruit and milk (soy, almond, cow's milk, hemp, or rice) and whatever else you feel like throwing in the blender! They are good for a snack or as a replacement of a meal if you're in a hurry. Here are two quick smoothies that make a nutritious treat any time of day.

Chocolate Almond Smoothie

Nuts and chocolate — I can't think of a more delicious food and flavor combination when it comes to desserts and special treats. If you're nuts about both like me, this is a keeper because it's like a chocolate milkshake, only better!

Single serving
Total time 5 minutes

1 frozen, peeled banana
1 cup (8 oz) almond milk
½ Tbsp chocolate syrup
10 raw almonds
½ frozen banana
Dash cinnamon and cocoa powder

1 Combine all ingredients in a blender and blend until smooth.

Note *If you don't have a frozen banana and/or like it colder, add a few ice cubes.*

Nutrition Snapshot
Per smoothie: 300 calories, 12g fat, 1g saturated fat, 6g protein, 45g carbs, 6g fiber, 170mg sodium

Preppy Probiotic Shake

This pretty pink smoothie has a little green surprise. It looks great, but more importantly, it has such a refreshing, unexpected taste from the combination of detoxifying herbs and a little added sweetness from the intense lemon curd. Kefir is a little-known, potent probiotic yogurt drink that is good for your immune system and gastrointestinal tract. It also helps with weight management. For some, it's an acquired taste, but kefir is really a beneficial food I hope you come to love!

Single serving
Total time 5 minutes

1 cup frozen strawberries
1 cup (8 oz) plain kefir
2 leaves fresh basil
1 Tbsp chopped fresh parsley
1 ½ tsp Lemon Curd, or substitute 1 Tbsp lemon juice + 2 tsp sugar

1 Combine all ingredients in a blender and blend until smooth.

Note *If you don't have a frozen banana and/or like it colder, add a few ice cubes.*

Nutrition Snapshot
Per shake: 220 calories, 5g fat, 2g saturated fat,
15g protein, 33g carbs, 6g fiber, 140mg sodium

Vegetarian Gluten Free

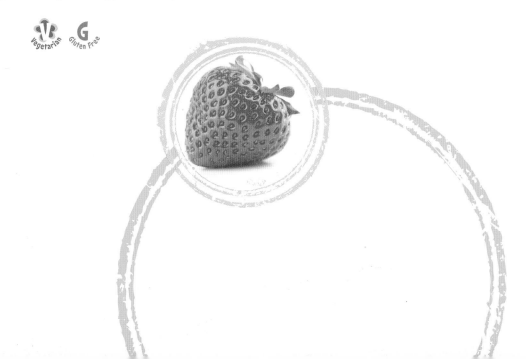

Whether for lunch or dinner, soups are a classic comfort food and a mainstay of healthy winter meals. These soups are recommended all year long particularly as 2-Week Challenge recipes. Big batches of soup take away the stress of daily planning and leftovers can be frozen for future meals. Make a large pot of any of these recipes and eat it for lunch, dinner or both throughout the week. I strongly suggest you invest in an immersion blender if you don't have one. They make blending soup a breeze. Soups are a fail-safe way to experiment with variety and seasonings and a great way to use up leftover vegetables and grains. Don't be afraid to get creative and have fun with your own versions!

Chapter 6

Slimming
Soups

Try It, You'll Like It Turkey Chili

This chili is fantastic in winter when fresh tomatoes aren't plentiful. Canned tomatoes are convenient and provide lycopene and vitamin C, which have been shown to be beneficial for eye health and cancer prevention.

7 Servings
Total time 30 minutes

3 Tbsp olive oil

1 lb ground turkey breast (or lean ground beef)

2 Tbsp chili powder

1 tsp cumin

½ Tbsp cinnamon

1 large red onion, chopped

1 bell pepper, chopped (any color)

3 (14.5-oz) cans diced no-salt-added tomatoes

1 (15-oz) can black beans, rinsed

½ tsp ground black pepper

½ tsp salt

1   Heat olive oil in large pot over medium-high heat.

2   Add turkey meat. Brown meat while stirring it and breaking it up with a wooden spoon or spatula.

3   Add all seasonings (chili powder, cinnamon, cumin, salt and pepper) as well as chopped onion and peppers. Cook 10 minutes or until onions are soft.

4   Add tomatoes and black beans and bring to boil.

5   Reduce heat to low and let chili simmer for 10 minutes. Season to taste. Remove from heat and serve.

Serving Tip   Add chopped avocado chunks on top. Kids love it with crushed multigrain tortilla chips and shredded cheddar cheese on top.

Menu Suggestion   Serve alone or over brown rice with Standby Green Salad (p. 74).

Nutrition Snapshot

Per 1 cup serving: 230 calories, 7g fat, 1g saturated fat, 20g protein, 21g carbs, 6g fiber, 470mg sodium

Spicy Quinoa, Black Bean, and Mushroom Soup

This poor man's soup is rich in nutrients and flavor. It's a 2-Week Challenge "must," but you're sure to adopt it as a favorite soup to have for any meal (maybe even breakfast?) and any season. It can stand alone, or be accompanied by any green salad.

10 **servings**
Total time 30 minutes

1 cup uncooked quinoa
1 can black beans, rinsed
2 Tbsp olive oil
1 (14.5-oz) container Mirepoix (or 1 cup each chopped carrots, onion, and celery)
2 cloves garlic, peeled and chopped
1 Tbsp finely chopped fresh ginger
2 cups sliced mushrooms (recommend baby bellas, also called criminis)
1 tsp salt
6 or 7 cups water
1 tsp hot pepper sauce
Lemon juice (optional)

1 Rinse quinoa well with cold water in a mesh wire sieve and set aside. (Note: The exact amount of quinoa will not affect this recipe.)

2 In a large pot or soup pot, heat 2 Tbsp olive oil and add Mirepoix, garlic, and ginger. Let cook until onions are soft.

3 Add mushrooms, quinoa, salt, and water. Bring to a boil, then reduce temperature and let simmer about 15 minutes.

4 Add black beans and a dash or more of hot sauce. Let cook on low heat about 10 more minutes.

5 Season with more hot sauce or salt and pepper as desired. Squeeze fresh lemon juice on top just before serving.

Note This soup becomes more stew-like as it sits. Add more water or broth (about 1 cup) and adjust seasoning according to taste.

Menu Suggestion Standby Green Salad (p. 74)

Nutrition Snapshot

Per 1 cup serving: 185 calories, 5g fat, 0.5g saturated fat, 6.5g protein, 28g carbs, 5.5 fiber, 510mg sodium

Hearty "Hamburger" Soup

Kids prefer this version of beef barley since it uses ground meat instead of beef chunks. It's one of my go-to, easy winter meals that I know my entire family will eat, and it leaves plenty of leftovers for lunch the next day. It's a perfect combination of protein, fiber, good carbs, and vitamins, but the real reason to eat it is great taste!

12 **servings**
Total time 30 minutes

1 lb 90% or leaner ground beef or ground turkey breast

1 (14.5-oz) container Mirepoix (or 1 cup each chopped carrots, onion, and celery)

3 Tbsp olive oil

1 tsp dried thyme

¼ cup chopped fresh parsley

3 cups low-sodium beef or chicken broth (vegetable broth can also be used)

3-4 cups water

1 (28-oz) can Low-Fat Tuscano Marinara Sauce

¾ cup jasmine brown rice

2 or 3 bay leaves

½ tsp salt

Pepper to taste

Grated Parmesan cheese (optional and omit during 2-Week Challenge)

1 Brown ground beef or turkey in a small pan and set aside. (If using beef, drain fat after browning).

2 Pour olive oil in a soup pot. Add Mirepoix and cook with thyme and parsley in soup pot until softened.

3 Add turkey and stir, then add all remaining ingredients except cheese. Cover and simmer on low heat about 45 minutes, until brown rice swells.

4 Serve immediately or refrigerate and heat as desired. Sprinkle some Parmesan cheese on top before serving as desired.

Note Rice may continue to soak up liquid, so you can add water or broth as needed before reheating. Barley or regular brown rice can be used instead of jasmine brown rice. Try adding some other veggies too, such as leeks, parsnips, turnips, or other.

G Gluten Free **Choose gluten-free broth**

Menu Suggestion Standby Green Salad (p. 74) and 1 multigrain roll per person

Nutrition Snapshot

Per serving: 210 calories, 8.5g fat, 2g saturated fat, 12g protein, 17g carbs, 3g fiber, 300mg sodium

Garden Goodness Soup or "Happy Accident"

Sometimes the best recipes come from "throwing it all in there," which is exactly how this recipe came about. I hate to waste food, particularly fresh produce. I think this recipe is perfect as is, but don't be afraid to toss in any veggies that might be on the verge of going bad if you don't use them. If you have a large soup pot, make this with the entire bag of arugula or broccoli slaw. A variety of veggies means lots of vitamins and minerals, but the best part is how delicious this simple soup is. It can stand alone or be served with a warm seeded roll and salad if you feel the need for even more green.

8 **Servings**
Total time 30-35 minutes

1 (14.5-oz) container Mirepoix (or 1 cup each chopped carrots, onion, and celery)
2 Tbsp butter
1 (10-oz) pkg asparagus, ends removed, cut in 1 inch pieces
½ (6-oz) pkg Wild Arugula
½ (12-oz) pkg Broccoli Slaw
4 cloves garlic, peeled and cut in half
2 cartons (64 oz) low sodium chicken broth
3 oz crème fraîche
1 tsp salt
¼ tsp ground black pepper

1   Melt butter in a large pot over medium heat and add Mirepoix. Let cook until softened, about 3 or 4 minutes.

2   Add asparagus, arugula, slaw, and garlic.

3   Pour in chicken broth to cover all vegetables. Bring to a boil, then reduce heat to simmer (medium-low heat) 25 minutes.

4   Remove from heat, and using an immersion blender, blend soup until very smooth.

5   Stir in crème fraîche, salt, and pepper. Return to low heat to keep warm before serving. Serve immediately or let cool and then refrigerate.

Menu Suggestion Standby Green Salad (p. 74)

Nutrition Snapshot
Per 1 cup serving: 85 calories, 3g fat, 2g saturated fat, 5g protein, 9g carbs, 3g fiber, 400mg sodium

Gluten Free
Choose gluten-free broth

Vegetarian
Use vegetable broth

Pumpkin Basil Soup

I'm known for always having canned pumpkin in my pantry. Even though pumpkin is a seasonal food, it's one you can stock up on. Keep extra cans of pumpkin purée to have for soups, scones, muffins, or favorite recipes whenever cravings strike. Powerful phytochemicals are packed in this delicious soup, and pepitas add a rich source of magnesium, potassium, iron, zinc, selenium, good fats (needed to help absorb the fat-soluble vitamins), fiber, and protein.

8 Servings
Total time 30 minutes

1 (15-oz) can pumpkin purée
1 large onion, peeled and finely chopped
3 Tbsp butter or Earth Balance
1 (28-oz) can whole tomatoes
¼ cup fresh chopped basil (or more)
½ tsp salt
¼ tsp pepper
3 large carrots, peeled and chopped
5 cups low sodium chicken broth (vegetable broth for vegetarian version)
½ tsp salt
Pepitas and more fresh basil for garnish

1 In large soup pot, cook onion in butter about 4 to 5 minutes. Add juice from canned tomatoes, then chop tomatoes and add with basil, salt, and pepper. Simmer gently about 10 more minutes.

2 In second small saucepan, simmer carrots in 2 ½ cups of chicken broth until soft.

3 Using an immersion blender, blend carrots and broth until puréed. Alternatively, pour soft carrots and broth into a blender or food processor and blend. Use extreme caution when blending hot soups.

4 Add canned pumpkin and blend until smooth. Add remaining chicken broth as necessary.

5 Add pumpkin mixture to tomatoes and onions. Season with ½ tsp salt and dash of pepper if needed. Thin with more chicken broth as desired.

6 Pour into soup tureen or individual bowls and top with ½ Tbsp pepitas per serving and fresh basil. Serve immediately.

Menu Suggestion Standby Green Salad (p. 74)

Gluten Free Choose gluten-free broth

Vegetarian Use vegetable broth

Nutrition Snapshot

Per 2 cup serving: 130 calories, 6g fat, 3g saturated fat, 4.5g protein, 15g carbs, 3g fiber, 520mg sodium

Corny Crab Chowder

You can't live in New England and not love a good, creamy chowda! After four years living there, I took that love of chowder with me. Making it myself, I had to come up with a less guilt-ridden yet equally decadent-tasting version. My goal was to make a rich and satisfying soup to warm you, fill you, and keep your energy up without weighing you down with too much fat and too many calories. Organic Russet Potatoes work best in this soup because they don't get mushy. For the record, potatoes are a high-potassium, high-fiber, nutritious food that still belong in your diet.

8 **Servings**
Total time 25 minutes

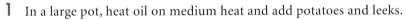

8 oz fresh crab meat or refrigerated canned crab meat
2 Tbsp olive oil
5-6 russet potatoes, peeled and cut in small chunks
2 leeks (1 pkg), sliced in thin rounds
1 ½ boxes (48 oz) low sodium chicken broth
1 ½ cups frozen corn
¼ tsp crushed red pepper
3-4 cubes frozen basil (optional)
½ cup half and half
½ tsp salt
¼ tsp pepper
Chopped fresh parsley or dried oregano to garnish

1 In a large pot, heat oil on medium heat and add potatoes and leeks.

2 Stir and cook potatoes and leeks until leeks are softened, about 3 or 4 minutes.

3 Add broth and let cook for 20 minutes.

4 Stir in crab, corn, red pepper, basil, half and half, salt, and pepper. Cook on low heat another 5 minutes.

5 Can serve immediately, topped with parsley or oregano.

Menu Suggestion Standby Green Salad (p. 74) and a multigrain roll

Nutrition Snapshot
Per 1 cup serving: 200 calories, 7g fat, 1.5g saturated fat,
13g protein, 18g carbs, 3g fiber, 320mg sodium

 Choose gluten-free broth

Chicken Tortellini Soup

Chicken soup hits the spot on a cold, gray winter days. This quick version has all the flavor and is packed with plenty of veggies to boost your immune system. I don't call it a "2-Week Challenge" recipe simply because of the tortellini, but they're certainly not banned from your diet entirely. After the challenge, this soup is a low-calorie, high-nutrient way to enjoy a little tortellini.

8 **Servings**
Total time 25 minutes

6 frozen chicken tenderloins
3 Tbsp olive oil, divided
3 large cloves garlic, minced
1 (14.5-oz) container Mirepoix (or 1 cup each chopped carrots, onion, and celery)
8 cups low sodium chicken broth
½ (12-oz) pkg Italian Tortellini with Mixed Cheese Filling (tri-color)
½ (8-oz) bag frozen petite peas
6 cups organic spinach
½ tsp salt, divided
¼ tsp pepper, divided
Grated Parmesan cheese (optional)

1   In a medium frying pan, heat 1 Tbsp oil over medium heat and add chicken. Sprinkle with ¼ tsp salt and ⅛ tsp pepper and brown on both sides, 3 to 4 minutes per side. Set aside.

2   In a soup pot, heat remaining oil; add garlic and Mirepoix. Let cook a few minutes until onions are soft. Add broth.

3   Bring broth to a boil and add tortellini. Let cook 5 minutes. (Do not overcook tortellini.)

4   Add peas, spinach, and remaining salt and pepper. Stir and bring to a simmer. Turn off heat.

5   Cut chicken in small pieces and add to soup.

6   Serve immediately with grated Parmesan cheese, or let cool and refrigerate.

Menu Suggestion Standby Green Salad (p. 74)

Nutrition Snapshot
Per 1 cup serving: 130 calories, 5g fat, 0.5g saturated fat, 11g protein, 9g carbs, 2.5g fiber, 225mg sodium

Ahhh, salad! This word should conjure up colorful images and make your mouth water at the thought of all the amazing tastes, textures, and variety. The days of iceberg and the anemic tomato wedge with bottled creamy dressing are long gone. If you haven't discovered today's offerings of salad varieties, say hello to a whole new world of rich greens and fresh foods that will help you lose weight and keep it off for life.

In order to lighten up, you must first be enlightened — and that means looking at salads in a whole new light. View them as your favorite part of the meal or as the main meal and not just the occasional "sometimes" side salad.

Work your way through this chapter, and you'll find you're having fun assembling scrumptious salads and creating your own favorite versions. Once you adopt salads as a daily staple, they do become a pleasurable habit and a necessary part of your diet, because they can keep you healthy, vibrant, and energetic.

Mix up greens and lettuces and toss with the same or various toppings daily. Even if you have no veggies or other additions, the greens alone with the dressing make a perfect accompaniment that fills you up. Bulk up your dinner daily with easy green salads.

One element of my salad recipes that might seem like more work (but really isn't) is the emphasis on homemade dressings. I never use a commercial dressing. When you get in the habit of tossing your salad with my mix of good oil, vinegars or lemon juice and the right seasonings, you won't go back to the bottle. The dressings with cheese can be made without it during the 2-Week Challenge, and then slowly restored after that. Cheese is not "verboten." Eat it mindfully and enjoy it!

The goal: Fill up on salad at least once or twice a day, and you really will keep the weight at bay.

Chapter 7

A Salad A Day

Standby Spinach, Mâche, Mixed Green, or Leafy Salad

This standby salad accompanies my dinner every day. I always keep fresh, organic baby spinach, mâche, arugula, mixed greens, and other bags of organic greens and lettuces in my fridge. Ready-to-use bagged lettuce leaves really are the best thing since sliced bread. The crunch of a simple salad goes with everything. It adds fiber and water to your meal, which helps with weight loss and maintenance.

2 **servings**
Total time 5 minutes

1 (6-oz) bag spinach or mixed greens
1 or 2 tomatoes, or 1 cup sliced grape or cherry tomatoes
½ cup shredded carrots (optional)
¼ cup sunflower seeds (optional)

I have a standard way of dressing most salads unless otherwise stated. I sprinkle the salad with a little bit (not measured) of TJ's garlic powder, sea salt, and black pepper. Then I drizzle TJ's extra virgin olive oil and either vinegar or lemon juice for an acid.
Toss salad until covered evenly with dressing. Serve immediately.

Note You may need to measure the dressing ingredients the first few times until you get a feel for the amounts. Start with these measurements:

Standard Dressing

⅛ tsp garlic powder
⅛ tsp sea salt
⅛ tsp black pepper
2 Tbsp olive oil

2 Tbsp one of the following:
Balsamic vinegar
White balsamic vinegar
Rice vinegar
Lemon juice

Nutrition Snapshot
Per 3-cup serving with standard dressing: 170 calories, 14g fat, 2g saturated fat, 3g protein, 10g carbs, 3g fiber, 280mg sodium

Vegetarian Gluten Free

Spinach Salad Nouveau

A spinach salad doesn't need bacon to justify its existence. I choose to add a roasted nut for good fats and added crunch. This salad can be eaten as a main course for two or serve four as a side salad.

2 **Servings**
Total time 15 minutes

1 (6-oz) bag organic baby spinach
¼ cup roasted hazelnuts, skins removed (or other nut)
2 hard-cooked eggs
1 large tomato, cut in chunks
⅛ tsp garlic powder
⅛ tsp salt
Pepper as desired
2 Tbsp rice vinegar
2 Tbsp olive oil

1 Roast hazelnuts as per instructions below.

2 Wash spinach and put in serving bowl. Add nuts, egg and tomato.

3 Sprinkle with salt, pepper, and garlic powder. Drizzle with vinegar and olive oil. Toss until thoroughly combined and serve immediately.

Roasting hazelnuts Preheat oven to 375°F. Place nuts on baking tray and put in the oven for 8 minutes. Remove immediately and place in kitchen towel. Rub to remove skins. Roasting brings out the great flavor of hazelnuts.

Nutrition Snapshot
Per half salad: 340 calories, 28g fat, 4g saturated fat, 10g protein, 10g carbs, 4g fiber, 320mg sodium

Festive Spinach Salad

If you're looking for a different spin on spinach salad, this is it! It can be a meal by itself or the perfect accompaniment to liven up grilled chicken or spaghetti marinara.

6 **servings**
Total time 6 minutes

2 (6-oz) bags baby spinach
1 cup frozen petite peas, rinsed with water to thaw slightly
1 cup chopped red bell pepper
¼ cup pine nuts or sunflower seeds
¼ cup canned white kidney beans or chick peas (optional)
⅓ cup refrigerated Genova Pesto
2 Tbsp white balsamic vinegar
⅛ tsp salt
Pepper to taste

1 Wash spinach and put in serving bowl.

2 Add peas, chopped pepper, nuts, and beans.

3 Toss well with pesto and vinegar. Sprinkle with salt and pepper if needed. Serve immediately.

Nutrition Snapshot
Per serving: 130 calories, 9g fat, 0g saturated fat,
4g protein, 9g carbs, 3g fiber, 100mg sodium

"Fly Me to the Moon" Arugula Salad

I love the British term for arugula. They call it "rocket," which I guess they stole from the French, who call it *"roquette."* I love arugula's peppery flair. Nutritionally speaking, this salad is a powerhouse of vitamins, minerals, and phytochemicals. Arugula is a natural food aphrodisiac as well, so you're going to feel extra good when you eat it (maybe that's the real reason the British call it rocket…)!

4 **Servings**
Total time 5 minutes

6 cups arugula
3 plum tomatoes, cut in quarters
¼ cup sunflower seeds
¼ cup grated fresh Parmesan cheese

1   Combine arugula, tomatoes, seeds and cheese in serving bowl.

2   Season and toss with Standard Balsamic Dressing (p. 74) or Creamy Balsamic Dressing (see below).

<u>Creamy Balsamic Vinaigrette</u>
1/3 cup balsamic vinegar
1/3 cup olive oil
1-2 cloves garlic, peeled
1 Tbsp Dijon mustard
1/3 tsp sugar
1/3 tsp salt

1   Whisk together vinaigrette ingredients.

Nutrition Snapshot *(Using Standard Balsamic Dressing)*
Per serving: 150 calories, 12g fat, 2g saturated fat, 5g protein, 6g carbs, 2g fiber, 180mg sodium

Vegetarian   Gluten Free

Red and Green Salad — Roasted Beets, Pomegranate, Red Onion, and Basil

This mix of purple, red and green is both beautiful and bursting with nutrition. It's a good example of how cheese can be enjoyed sparingly and mindfully. Of course, the salad is flavorful and even lower in fat and calories without it.

4 **Servings**
Total time 5 minutes

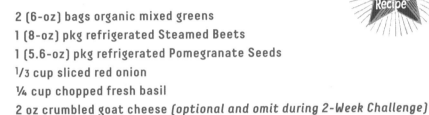 Omit goat cheese

2 (6-oz) bags organic mixed greens
1 (8-oz) pkg refrigerated Steamed Beets
1 (5.6-oz) pkg refrigerated Pomegranate Seeds
1/3 cup sliced red onion
¼ cup chopped fresh basil
2 oz crumbled goat cheese (*optional and omit during 2-Week Challenge*)

1 Combine all salad ingredients in a large bowl and toss with Standard Dressing (p. 74) using white balsamic vinegar. Serve immediately.

Nutrition Snapshot
Per serving: 180 calories, 11g fat, 3g saturated fat, 6g protein, 18g carbs, 5g fiber, 240mg sodium

Favorite Summer Salad

This enhanced version of an Insalata Caprese is so good, you may want to make it your meal for lunch or dinner or both every day in summer. Serve it with a warm, crispy seeded roll for what I call a perfect (vegetarian) meal.

4 **Servings**
Total time 8 minutes

2 avocados, peeled and cut into chunks
3 or 4 tomatoes, chopped into small wedges (or use plum or cherry tomatoes)
1 seedless cucumber, peeled and cut into chunks
4 oz fresh mozzarella, cut in small chunks
¼ cup fresh basil leaves, cut up (more if desired)
⅛ tsp garlic powder
¼ tsp salt
⅛ tsp pepper
2 Tbsp olive oil
3 Tbsp balsamic vinegar

1 Combine avocado, tomato, cucumber, cheese, and basil in a bowl.

2 Season with salt, pepper, and garlic powder.

3 Drizzle with oil and vinegar and toss well to coat. Serve immediately, or refrigerate for about an hour or more before serving.

Nutrition Snapshot

Per serving: 270 calories, 22g fat, 5g saturated fat,
10g protein, 11g carbs, 6g fiber, 330mg sodium

Watercress Salad with Goat Cheese, Mango, and Honey-Lime Vinaigrette

The idea of this salad came to me while I was daydreaming about Provence and how much I love the goat cheese there. Two nutritional reasons to eat watercress salad are calcium and vitamin C. If you don't have watercress, try mâche (lamb's lettuce).

4 **Servings**
Total time 8 minutes

1 large bunch watercress
1 mango or 1 (12-oz) pkg sliced Fresh Mango
4 oz fresh goat cheese

1 Wash watercress well and put in shallow serving dish or spread onto salad plate.

2 Peel and cut mango into strips or chunks and distribute over watercress.

3 Crumble or cut 1 oz goat cheese onto each salad.

4 Drizzle Honey-Lime Vinaigrette (see below) on salad and serve immediately.

Honey-Lime Vinaigrette
1 Tbsp honey
Juice of 2 fresh limes
¼ cup olive oil
¼ tsp salt

1 Whisk together vinaigrette ingredients.

Nutrition Snapshot
Per serving: 250 calories, 20g fat, 6g saturated fat,
7g protein, 14g carbs, 1g fiber, 260mg sodium

Vegetarian   Gluten Free

Great Greek Salad

A true summer favorite with fresh herbs, this variation on the classic version adds great flavor, texture, fiber and protein with the garbanzo beans. It's not just my favorite summer salad, it's always a hit for summertime grilling and parties.

4 **Servings**
Total time 10 minutes

2 or 3 large tomatoes cut in wedges, or 1 cup cherry tomatoes cut in halves
1 seedless cucumber, peeled and cut in chunks
1 yellow bell pepper, cored and cut in small chunks
1 cup garbanzo beans, drained
4 oz feta cheese
¼ cup black olives, pitted and cut in half
¼ cup fresh mint leaves, chopped
¼ cup fresh oregano leaves, chopped
2 lemons
2 Tbsp olive oil
Pepper to taste (no salt needed)

1 Combine veggies, beans, cheese, olives, and herbs in serving bowl.

2 Cut and squeeze lemons through a strainer onto salad.

3 Pour oil on salad, toss to combine, and season with pepper.

4 Serve immediately or refrigerate up to an hour before serving.

Nutrition Snapshot
Per serving: 170 calories, 11g fat, 2g saturated fat,
6g protein, 17g carbs, 5g fiber, 280mg sodium

Bitter, Sweet, and Nutty Salad

This is like having dinner and dessert all in one. Sweet and salty, nutty and crunchy, nutritious and delicious -- a salad that's All Good!

4 **Servings**
Total time 5 minutes

 **Omit honey**

1 (7-oz) bag Butter Lettuce and Radicchio
1 cup frozen Roasted Corn, thawed
½ (8-oz) pkg refrigerated Steamed Beets
¼ cup chopped fresh parsley
¼ cup chopped raw pecans
¼ tsp salt
⅛ tsp pepper
⅛ tsp garlic power

1 Combine all ingredients together in large salad bowl and toss with Sweet and Tangy Dressing (see below).

Sweet and Tangy Dressing
2 Tbsp olive oil
2 Tbsp balsamic vinegar
1 Tbsp rice vinegar
1 Tbsp Dijon mustard
1 tsp honey (omit during 2-Week Challenge)

1 Whisk together dressing ingredients.

Nutrition Snapshot
Per serving: 160 calories, 12g fat, 1g saturated fat, 2g protein, 13g carbs, 2g fiber, 240mg sodium

 Vegetarian G Gluten Free

Move Over Cobb, It's Melt-in-Your-Mouth Mâche Salad

No egg or blue cheese here, but you won't miss them or all those extra calories from a traditional, heavy Cobb Salad. This meal of a salad will truly melt in your mouth and put a smile on your face!

2 **Servings**
Total time 6 minutes

1 bag Mâche (lamb's lettuce)
3 slices Fully Cooked Uncured Bacon
½ avocado, sliced
⅓ cup garbanzo beans, rinsed
¼ cup salted cashews
⅓ tsp each, salt, garlic powder, and pepper
1 lemon
2 Tbsp olive oil

1 Heat bacon according to package instructions.

2 Add mâche to a large salad bowl. Add avocado chunks and garbanzos.

3 Crumble bacon onto salad and toss on cashews.

4 Sprinkle with seasonings, then squeeze juice of lemon on salad, drizzle with olive oil, and toss well together. Divide salad between two plates and serve immediately.

Nutrition Snapshot
Per serving: 370 calories, 30g fat, 5g saturated fat, 11g protein, 19g carbs, 7g fiber, 600mg sodium

  Omit bacon

Double Bean and Basil Salad

There is no better flavor combination than tomatoes and basil. When you mix them with white beans and lemons, the flavor truly explodes! If you aren't a fan of raw onions, simply omit them from the salad. The cucumber adds crunch, and creamy avocado just makes it all melt together.

6 **Servings**
Total time 8 minutes

1 (15-oz) can white kidney (cannellini) beans, rinsed and drained
1 (15-oz) can red kidney beans, rinsed and drained
1 cup sliced cherry tomatoes (or use small vine-ripened tomatoes or grape tomatoes)
¼ cup thinly sliced red onion
1 large seedless cucumber, peeled and chopped
¼ cup chopped fresh basil
¼ tsp salt
⅛ tsp pepper
⅛ tsp garlic powder
Juice of 2 or 3 lemons
2 Tbsp olive oil

1   Combine beans, tomatoes, onion, cucumber, and basil in a serving bowl.

2   Sprinkle with seasonings, then squeeze on lemon juice and drizzle olive oil.

3   Toss well to dress evenly and serve. Can be refrigerated for several hours before serving.

Nutrition Snapshot
Per serving: 175 calories, 5g fat, 0.5g saturated fat,
9g protein, 26g carbs, 11g fiber, 280mg sodium

It's Slawsome!

Cabbage deserves royal treatment, because it's the king of the cruciferous vegetables when it comes to cancer-fighting phytochemicals. Thanks to the lime and sunflower seeds, this salad is a light and crunchy yet rich and decadent winning weight-loss combo. With or without cilantro (for the non-cilantro crowd) this may be the most enjoyable cabbage on earth!

4 Servings
Total time 5 minutes

. . . .

1 (10-oz) bag Shredded Cabbage
1/3 cup Parmesan (or Pecorino) cheese
¼ cup sunflower seeds
4 chopped scallions
¼ cup cilantro
2 Tbsp cup olive oil
2 Tbsp white balsamic vinegar
1 large or 2 small limes (lemon can substituted)
¼ tsp sea salt
Pepper as desired

1 Combine cabbage, cheese, seeds, scallions, and cilantro in a large bowl.

2 In a small bowl whisk together oil, vinegar, lime juice, salt, and pepper.

3 Pour dressing over slaw and toss well to completely cover slaw with dressing.

4 Serve immediately or, better yet, refrigerate for at least an hour to allow flavors to meld.

Nutrition Snapshot

Per 1 cup serving: 190 calories, 13g fat, 2g saturated fat,
6g protein, 13g carbs, 3g fiber, 270mg sodium

Vegetarian Gluten Free

Thai-Me Broccoli Slaw

I typically make this slaw with shredded red and green cabbage, but the red cabbage went missing from TJ's, and the broccoli slaw was just begging for attention. The result is a colorful, low-calorie, nutrient-packed slaw that keeps you coming back for more. It's loaded with vitamins and antioxidants, so go for it!

6 **Servings**
Total time 10 minutes

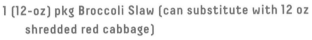

Omit brown sugar

1 (12-oz) pkg Broccoli Slaw (can substitute with 12 oz
 shredded red cabbage)
1 ½ cups chopped red bell pepper
1 carrot, peeled and cut in small chunks
¼ cup chopped fresh cilantro
¼ cup chopped fresh basil (optional)

1 Combine all ingredients together and toss well with Spicy Peanut Dressing (see below).

<u>Spicy Peanut Dressing</u>
¼ cup rice wine vinegar
1 Tbsp reduced sodium soy sauce
1 Tbsp sesame oil
2 Tbsp smooth natural peanut butter
1 ½ tsp brown sugar *(omit during 2-Week Challenge)*
1 clove garlic, peeled and crushed, or ½ tsp garlic powder
1 tsp red pepper flakes
½ tsp salt

1 Whisk together dressing ingredients.

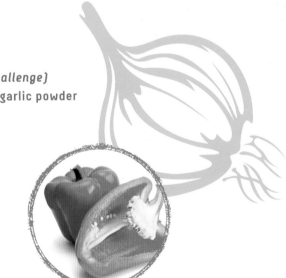

Nutrition Snapshot
Per 1 cup serving: 100 calories, 6g fat, 1g saturated fat,
4g protein, 9g carbs, 3g fiber, 330mg sodium

 Vegetarian **Gluten Free** Use gluten-free soy sauce

Love Me Lentil Salad

I call this dish a salad, but it's hearty enough to double as a side dish, lunch, or even dinner. Add an ounce of smoked gouda, and it's all you need to fill yourself up, cheer yourself up, and keep your energy up for hours.

4 **Servings**
Total time 10 minutes

1 (17.6-oz) pkg refrigerated Steamed Lentils
3 carrots, peeled and diced
1/3 cup kalamata olives, pitted and sliced
4 scallions, ends removed and finely sliced
½ small fennel bulb, chopped
2 Tbsp chopped fresh dill (or 2 tsp dried)
2 Tbsp chopped fresh oregano (or 2 tsp dried)
1 clove garlic, minced
2 Tbsp balsamic vinegar
¼ cup olive oil extra virgin
Juice of 2 fresh lemons
¼ tsp salt
1/8 tsp pepper

1 Mix all ingredients in a large bowl and chill.

2 Allow several hours or overnight for flavors to blend.
Bring to room temperature before serving. (Can also eat immediately.)

Note For added zing, squeeze fresh lemon juice over the dish before serving.

Nutrition Snapshot

Per 1 cup serving: 330 calories, 15g fat, 2g saturated fat, 12g protein, 35g carbs, 12g fiber, 600mg sodium

Loaded Black Bean Salad

Black beans are a usual suspect in Mexican fare, particularly when paired with corn, peppers, and cilantro. Give them a little Italian slant instead, and you will find that they are the best legume on arugula. Toss these few ingredients together for a winning weight-loss salad that's loaded with vitamins, fiber, phytochemicals, a little good fat, and great flavors. It's such a simple salad to assemble in minutes - great for lunch or side dish.

2 **Servings**
Total time 6 minutes

1 (15-oz) can black beans, rinsed
2 cups arugula
½ cup sliced grape or cherry tomatoes
½ cup chopped cucumber
1/3 cup thinly sliced red onion
1 cup chopped bell peppers (any color)
¼ tsp salt
1/3 tsp garlic powder
2 Tbsp white balsamic vinegar
1 Tbsp olive oil

1 Combine beans, arugula, tomatoes, and vegetables in a bowl.

2 Sprinkle with salt and garlic powder.

3 Drizzle with oil and vinegar and toss well before serving.

Note For added zing, squeeze fresh lemon juice over the dish before serving.

Nutrition Snapshot
Per 1.5 cup serving: 160 calories, 4g fat, 0g saturated fat,
6g protein, 25g carbs, 7g fiber, 500mg sodium

Asian Chopped Chicken Salad

When it comes to vegetables, anyone will admit cutting and chopping is a chore, and it often becomes the barrier that prevents many people from eating them. Then comes TJ's to the rescue with its ultra-time-saving foods such as the chopped veggie mix and cooked white meat chicken. Forget "fast food" of the past – here is some real fast food of our today!

2 **Servings**
Total time 5 minutes

1 (16-oz) pkg Healthy 8 Chopped Veggie Mix
6 oz Just Chicken white meat chicken
¼ cup sunflower seeds
¼ cup chopped fresh cilantro
1 or 2 limes

1 In a large bowl, combine veggie mix, chicken, seeds, and cilantro.

2 Cut limes and squeeze juice over salad mixture and toss.

3 Pour Asian Dressing (see below) over salad, toss evenly, and serve.

Asian Dressing
3 Tbsp rice vinegar
1 Tbsp sesame oil
¼ tsp salt
Dash black pepper

1 Whisk together dressing ingredients.

Nutrition Snapshot
*Per ½ salad serving: 370 calories, 18g fat, 3g saturated fat,
32g protein, 23g carbs, 7g fiber, 470mg sodium*

New Nicoise

Canned salmon is an easy and cost-effective way to get your DHA omega-3 fatty acids. Toss it on a bed of greens and enjoy this heart-healthy meal.

2 **Servings**
Total time 8 minutes

Omit sugar

1 (6-oz) can Wild Alaskan Pink Salmon
½ cup shelled edamame (fresh or frozen)
½ lb asparagus
2 hard-cooked eggs
½ cup sliced cherry tomatoes

1. Put salmon in glass or other serving bowl. Add edamame.

2. Slice about 1 inch off bottoms of asparagus. Place in a medium-sized shallow pan and add ¼ to ⅓ cup water. (You do not have to be precise.)

3. Place pan with asparagus on stove over high heat and bring to a boil. Cover and let cook/steam for just 2 minutes. Remove immediately and rinse with cold water.

4. Cut asparagus into smaller pieces and add to salmon.

5. Slice eggs into wedges and place on salmon.

6. Pour Balsamic Vinaigrette (see below) over salad. Serve on bed of greens if desired.

Balsamic Vinaigrette
3 Tbsp balsamic vinegar
2 Tbsp olive oil
1 clove garlic, peeled
1 Tbsp Dijon mustard
⅛ tsp sugar *(omit during 2-Week Challenge)*
⅛ tsp salt

1. Whisk together dressing ingredients.

Nutrition Snapshot
Per serving: 370 calories, 23g fat, 4g saturated fat, 33g protein, 9g carbs, 4g fiber, 570mg sodium

Gluten Free

Lunch is not necessarily different from dinner, but in the United States, we are so used to eating sandwiches and fast foods for lunch because so many of us don't have or don't make time to slow down and have a real mid-day meal. Whether at home, at work, or on the run, lunch is a meal that should not be skipped. Plan ahead the night before or allow for extra time in the morning, so you're not left lunch-less and ravenous! This chapter offers quick, nutritious sandwiches and other quick and easy food ideas. Use these recipes as a supplement to soups and salads, which are two things that always make an ideal daily lunch pairing. I encourage you to plan on a salad for lunch, particularly during the 2-Week Challenge.

Chapter 8
Lean Lunching

Sandwich Love

This sandwich should be known as the 2-Week Challenge Signature Sandwich.
I recommend it to all as a daily no-brainer, delicious, satisfying, and highly nutritious light lunch. It helps to ward off afternoon "lows" that lead to sugar cravings, earning its proven record as an "eat daily and lose weight" meal.

1 **Sandwich**
Total time 3 minutes

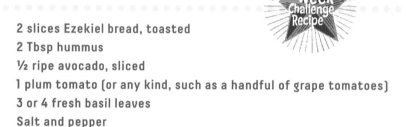

2 slices Ezekiel bread, toasted
2 Tbsp hummus
½ ripe avocado, sliced
1 plum tomato (or any kind, such as a handful of grape tomatoes)
3 or 4 fresh basil leaves
Salt and pepper

1 Spread hummus on both slices of toast.

2 Place avocado slices on top of hummus layer, then add tomato layer.

3 Add a dash of salt and pepper to each slice then top with fresh basil leaves.

4 Eat immediately and love it!

Nutrition Snapshot
Per sandwich: 330 calories, 14g fat, 1g saturated fat,
11g protein, 40g carbs, 13g fiber, 300mg sodium

Egg Salad Sandwich

You can hard-cook your own eggs or go the ultimate convenience route of buying them in a bag at TJ's. I have to admit, I love egg salad and the pre-cooked eggs make it faster than any fast food, and a whole lot healthier.

2 Sandwiches
Total time 5 minutes

6 hard-cooked eggs
1 finely chopped scallion
3 Tbsp mayo
¼ tsp pepper
¼ tsp garlic powder
½ cup arugula
1 tomato
2 slices Ezekiel bread

1 Using an egg-slicer or knife, cut egg into small slices/pieces and put in a small mixing bowl.

2 Add scallion, mayo, pepper and garlic powder and mix until eggs are moistened and well-blended.

3 Divide evenly and spread egg salad onto 2 slices Ezekiel bread (toasted if desired.)

4 Top with ½ tomato and ¼ cup arugula per sandwich. Cover with second slice of bread and enjoy.

Lunch Suggestion Serve with ½ cup Double Bean and Basil Salad (p. 92) or Love Me Lentil Salad (p. 98)

Nutrition Snapshot

Per sandwich: 480 calories, 24g fat, 6g saturated fat,
24g protein, 32g carbs, 7g fiber, 400mg sodium

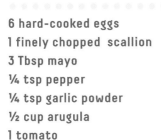

Southwest Chicken Patty

Occasionally you just want a burger. The frozen Grilled Chicken Burger Patty is a good choice when the urge strikes. I keep a package in my freezer for just such a time. Whip this burger together in minutes with a few of TJ's convenient foods and you realize how easy it is to make small changes that make a big difference to your health. (Compare nutrition info to a 1,000+ calorie Southwest-style restaurant burger sometime!)

Single serving
Total time 6 minutes

1 Grilled Chicken Burger Patty
½ cup frozen Organic Brown Rice
½ ripe avocado, sliced
3 Tbsp salsa (any variety)

1 Heat chicken patty and rice in microwave according to instructions.

2 Place rice on serving plate and top with warm chicken patty.

3 Slice avocado and place on top of chicken.

4 Top with salsa and eat immediately.

Serving Suggestion Enjoy with a small green salad and a glass of lemon seltzer with a splash of pomegranate juice.

Nutrition Snapshot
Per serving: 370 calories, 16g fat, 3g saturated fat, 28g protein, 27g carbs, 6g fiber, 550mg sodium

Tex-Mex Lunch Bowl

This hearty lunch bowl can be made vegetarian by replacing chicken with black or other beans, or simply leave out the chicken. I keep limes on hand for dishes like this because a little lime juice adds both flavor and vitamins with no calories.

Single serving
Total time 5 minutes

3 oz or ½ cup Just Chicken White Meat Chicken
½ cup frozen Organic Brown Rice, thawed according to instructions
½ cup frozen roasted corn, thawed
½ avocado, sliced
¼ red bell pepper, chopped
2-3 Tbsp fresh cilantro, chopped
1 lime
2 Tbsp Double Roasted Salsa (or any salsa you like)

1 Combine chicken, rice, corn, avocado, pepper, and cilantro in a bowl.

2 Cut lime and squeeze juice over chicken mixture and stir. Top with salsa before eating.

Nutrition Snapshot

Per serving: 410 calories, 14g fat, 2g saturated fat,
32g protein, 41g carbs, 8g fiber, 210mg sodium

Gluten Free

Quick Quesadillas

Thanks to these special whole grain tortillas, my kids and I often eat this nutritious, high-fiber lunch that is faster and healthier than any Tex-Mex drive-through.

2 Servings
Total time 10 minutes

4 Whole Grain Flour Tortillas with oats and flax
Canola spray
½ cup Traditional Style Fat-Free Refried Beans
1 cup frozen Fire Roasted Bell Peppers and Onions
½ cup (8 Tbsp) Fancy Shredded Lite Mexican Blend cheese

1 Spray medium-sized frying pan with canola spray and heat over low heat. Put tortilla in pan.

2 In a small pan, heat refried beans with peppers and onions until warm and beans are not thick and pasty. Peppers and onions should no longer be frozen.

3 Spoon half the bean and pepper mixture onto the tortilla.

4 Sprinkle 4 Tbsp cheese on top then place a second tortilla on top.

5 Turn heat up to medium and let cook 1 minute. Flip tortilla and cook 1 to 2 more minutes.

6 Remove from pan and repeat steps for second quesadilla.

Serving Suggestion Serve quesadillas with salsa, fat-free sour cream, or 1 Tbsp guacamole or avocado slices.

Nutrition Snapshot

Per quesadilla: 410 calories, 10g fat, 3g saturated fat,
21g protein, 63g carbs, 14g fiber, 700mg sodium

  Use brown rice tortilla

Chapter 9
Dinner's On

Dinner is the main American meal, but ideally, dinner should not provide the majority of anyone's daily calorie intake. This chapter focuses on healthy dinners that are lower in calories because they're based on best-sized portions of meats, fish, pasta, and vegetarian entrees. Many of these recipes can stand alone or be combined with great Sides to Slenderize (see chapter 10). 2-Week Challenge recipes are indicated. Many of the dishes include lots of veggies, yet I still recommend a salad with every dinner meal. Salads fill you up with low-calorie, high-water-content, nutrient-dense foods that won't weigh you down. If you've eaten enough dinner, the desire for dessert or evening-time snacking will diminish, and that's a very good thing!

Everyone Loves Pasta — The Scoop On Our Favorite Forbidden Carb

I dare you to say you don't love pasta! You may claim you don't, but that's probably because you have been brainwashed into thinking it's B-A-D. I'm telling you that's simply unfair! The words "pasta" and "bad" do not belong in the same sentence.

As a reminder, the body needs good, complex carbohydrates, and what I call "new and improved pastas" are just that. I cook strictly with whole grain versions, so even though I have not specifically written that in the recipes, that's what I recommend. Trader Joe's whole wheat pastas are my favorite, but don't feel limited by my selection. There are many available that have a good ratio of carbs to protein and some fiber to balance the simple carbs, and they still taste like pasta!

Here's a need-to-know tip about pasta: Cook it al dente (still a tad chewy) if you are concerned about the glycemic index. It has a lower glycemic load when slightly undercooked.

Pasta is excluded from the 2-Week Challenge because we all tend to eat too much of it. With pasta, we're used to being served a mountain that is often covered with heavy sauces and cheese. During the two weeks, cheese is off limits, and I want you to focus on having a salad with dinner every night, which helps cut down on portions of the main dish. Once the salads have become a habit, I find it's okay to bring pasta back into play but with a little more awareness of type (whole grain), portion, cooking method and accompaniments. That said, I am a big fan of pasta dishes, and they are what my family and I eat most frequently.

One final note: If you are athletic, these dishes are going to be great fuel for your body. Enjoy them and get rid of any guilt that may have been ingrained in you over the past "no carb" decade.

Bottom line: Dig into my pasta dishes and feel good about it!

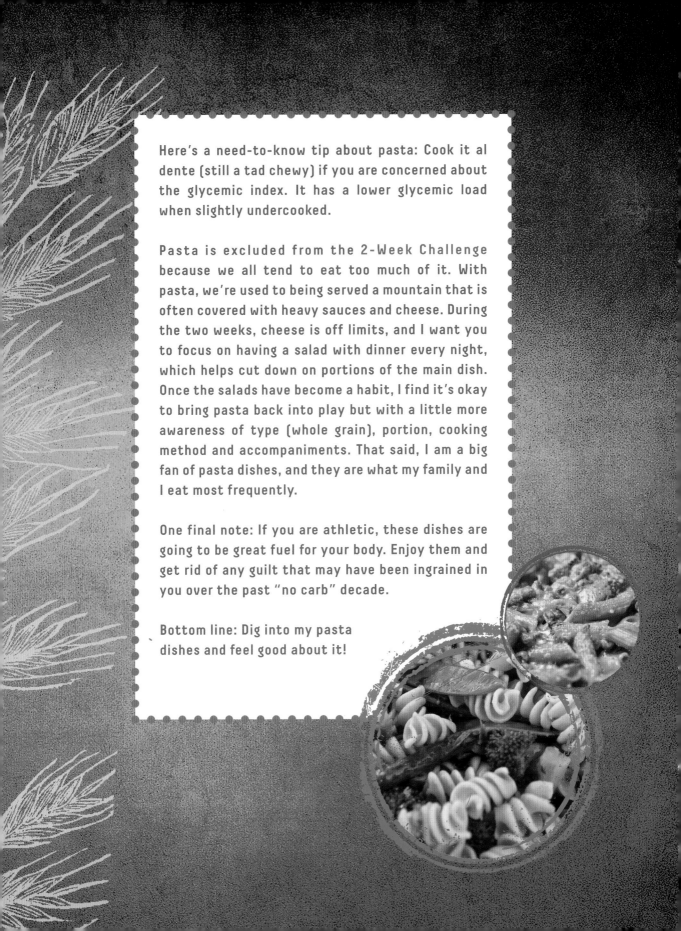

Best-Loved Chicken Balsamico

This balsamic-infused chicken has become a family favorite not only my family but for many of my friends' families too. It's always a crowd-pleaser, most likely because it's simplicity at its best! Leftover chicken makes a great cold sandwich or salad addition the next day.

My gourmet tip: Add shiitake (or other mushrooms) to the chicken for even tastier results!

4 **Servings**
Total time 20-25 minutes

4 (4 oz each) skinless, boneless chicken breasts

3 Tbsp olive oil

2 cloves garlic, minced

2 or 3 shallots, chopped

2/3 cup low sodium chicken broth

1/3 cup balsamic vinegar

½ tsp salt

Black pepper to taste

1 Heat oil in large frying pan on medium-high heat. Add chicken and brown on both sides.

2 Add garlic and shallots and cook until soft/tender.

3 Add broth, balsamic vinegar, and salt. Bring to a boil, then reduce heat and simmer uncovered 15 minutes or until liquid reduces and becomes thick and syrupy.

4 Season with pepper. Remove from heat and serve.

Note Chicken breasts vary in weight and size. Weigh them to get an idea of portion, or divide the weight on the package by the number of breasts. Each breast should weigh no more than 4 ounces, otherwise cut each in half.

Menu Suggestion Serve with Standby Green Salad (p. 74), Cumin Carrots (p. 176) and Sizzling Spuds with Sage (p. 187). Other great sides are asparagus, Brussels sprouts, or baby broccoli and brown rice or jasmine rice.

Nutrition Snapshot

Per serving: 190 calories, 9g fat, 1g saturated fat, 23g protein, 3g carbs, 0g fiber, 600mg sodium

 **Choose gluten-free broth**

Smothered in the Oven Chicken with Eggplant-Tomato Sauce

Chicken Parmesan meets Eggplant Parmesan and they go on a diet together. The result is this light, delicious, nutritious dish. If you're missing your vino on the 2-Week Challenge, here's a way to get a little red-wine flavor!

6 **Servings**
Total time 45minutes

6 (4 oz each) chicken breasts
3 Tbsp olive oil, divided
1 (14.5-oz) container Mirepoix (or 1 cup each chopped carrots, onion, and celery)
1 large eggplant, peeled and cubed
4 or 5 large cloves garlic, minced
1 (28-oz) can no-added-sodium diced tomatoes
½ cup red wine (TJ's "3 Buck Chuck" cabernet is fine)
¼ cup each, chopped fresh basil and Italian parsley
½ tsp salt and pepper to taste

1 Preheat oven to 350°F. Rinse chicken breasts and pat dry.

2 Heat 2 Tbsp oil over medium-high heat in a Dutch oven or oven-safe pan. When oil crackles, add chicken breasts and brown on each side, about 2-3 minutes per side. Remove from pan to a plate.

3 Add remaining oil and Mirepoix to pan and cook 2 minutes, then add eggplant.

4 Cook eggplant mix another 3 or 4 minutes, then add garlic. Stir and cook for 2 minutes.

5 Add tomatoes, red wine, basil, parsley, salt, and pepper. Slowly stir all ingredients until combined.

6 Return chicken to the Dutch oven and cover with sauce. Put lid on Dutch oven and place in oven for 30 minutes.

Note Leftover sauce can be used as pasta sauce or eaten on a bowl of quinoa or brown rice.

Menu Suggestion Serve with Standby Green Salad (p. 74), Quinoa, Organic Brown Rice, or Jasmine Rice is okay too if you're looking for a larger meal and good carb to go with it.

Nutrition Snapshot

Per serving: 250 calories, 8g fat, 1g saturated fat, 26g protein, 16g carbs, 5g fiber, 600mg sodium

Chicken, Southern Greens, and Beans

This recipe's for my little Southern mama who inspired me to cook things like this. She loved all greens, so I developed an open mind to them once I outgrew the adolescent who looked at them in disgust! To bean nay-sayers and those who call this "peasant food," I call it a "perfect dish" — easy to make and bursting with flavor and winning nutritional value. The greens and beans pack a lot of fiber, calcium, iron and vitamin A into one great meal. Oh, and my mom praised it — that's how I knew I had a keeper!

6 **Servings**
Total time 20 minutes

6 (4 oz each) skinless, boneless chicken breasts
2 Tbsp olive oil
2 shallots, peeled and chopped
1 (16-oz) bag Southern Greens Blend
3 Tbsp capers with liquid
1 cup low sodium chicken broth
1 (15-oz) can white kidney beans, rinsed (butter beans can be substituted, but
     they are not available at TJ's)
Pepper to taste (capers are salty, so sample before adding any salt)

1 Heat oil in an electric or stove-top skillet. Add chicken breasts and brown on both sides, roughly 3 minutes each side. Remove from pan to a plate.

2 Add shallots to the pan and cook for 2 minutes.

3 Add greens, capers, and broth. Cook 4 minutes or until greens are softened. (You may have to add ½ the greens, cook them down and then add the rest.)

4 Add chicken back to pan, reduce heat to low and let simmer 8 minutes.

5 Add beans and let cook another 2-3 minutes. Season and serve immediately.

Menu Suggestion Standby Green Salad (p. 74) and brown rice if desired. The dish alone is very filling and satisfying.

Nutrition Snapshot

Per serving: 250 calories, 8g fat, 1g saturated fat, 30g protein, 15g carbs, 7.5g fiber, 630mg sodium

 Choose gluten-free broth

Savory Sage Chicken with Butternut Squash and White Beans

White kidney beans, aka cannellini, are my personal favorite bean. Depending on the time of year, they can be paired with a variety of herbs and meat or vegetables. This is my favorite fall and wintertime combination. It's a colorful, flavorful and nutrient-rich single pan meal!

4 **Servings**
Total time 15 minutes

4 (4 oz each) skinless, boneless chicken breasts
2 Tbsp olive oil
2 cloves garlic, minced
10 or more large fresh sage leaves
½ tsp salt
1 cup low sodium chicken broth
2 cups pre-cut butternut squash
1 (15-oz) can cannellini beans, rinsed and drained
⅛ tsp pepper

1 In a large frying pan, heat oil and garlic on medium-high heat for about 1 minute, then add chicken breasts.

2 Place sage leaves on top and around chicken. Sprinkle with salt.

3 Brown the chicken on each side(about 3 minutes), then add chicken broth and butternut squash.

4 Bring to a boil, reduce heat to low, cover and let simmer 5-6 minutes.

5 Add beans to the pan, stir, and season with pepper. Serve immediately.

Menu Suggestion
Cooked quinoa or Organic Brown Rice and a large serving of Standby Green Salad (p. 74).

Nutrition Snapshot
Per serving: 290 calories, 8g fat, 1g saturated fat,
31g protein, 23g carbs, 9g fiber, 800mg sodium

 **Choose gluten-free broth**

Dutch Oven Dijon Chicken with New Potatoes

Many dieters said goodbye to potatoes long ago. The truth about our beloved spud is that it's a good starch loaded with potassium (more than bananas) and fiber. The cooking method used here creates a healthy "meat and potatoes" dish, and the portion does not go overboard.

4 **Servings**
Total time 40 minutes

4 (4 oz) skinless, boneless chicken breasts
2 Tbsp olive oil
3 shallots, peeled and sliced
½ tsp salt
¼ tsp black pepper
½ cup white wine
1 Tbsp Dijon mustard
4 lemons
1 (28-oz) bag Potato Medley

1 Preheat oven to 400°F.

2 Heat oil in Dutch oven or heavy oven-safe pot. Add shallots and chicken. Brown chicken on each side, roughly 3 minutes per side.

3 Sprinkle with salt and pepper. Add wine, mustard, and juice of lemons. Reserve the lemons and cut each half into quarters.

4 Slice potatoes in half and add with cut-up lemons to chicken.

5 Spoon liquid over potatoes and chicken, cover and put in heated oven. Bake 30 minutes.

Menu Suggestion Serve with Light and Lemony Lentils (p. 170) and Standby Green Salad (p. 74).

Nutrition Snapshot
*Per serving: 360 calories, 8.5g fat, 1g saturated fat,
28g protein, 46g carbs, 8.5g fiber, 740mg sodium*

Trini Chicken

I adapted this recipe from my sister-in-law who comes from Trinidad. She's a great cook, and the combination of flavors makes a savory, vitamin-rich sauce that is served best over quinoa to soak up the flavorful liquid.

4 **Servings**
Total time 40 minutes (after marinating)

Omit brown sugar

4 (4 oz) chicken breasts, rinsed and patted dry
4-5 cloves of garlic, minced
2 tsp finely chopped fresh ginger
2 Tbsp reduced sodium soy sauce
1 small onion, peeled and chopped
1 tsp each, dried thyme, basil, chive and oregano (2 Tbsp chopped fresh can be used for any)
3 Tbsp olive oil, divided
2 Tbsp brown sugar *(omit during 2-Week Challenge)*
2 medium tomatoes, chopped
1 sweet/bell pepper, chopped

1 Combine garlic, ginger, soy sauce, onion, herbs, and 2 Tbsp oil in a dish.

2 Add chicken and cover with marinade. Cover and let marinate for an hour — or all day if made early in the day or overnight.

3 Heat remaining 1 Tbsp oil in heavy pot on medium heat. Before oil gets hot, add sugar. As it heats, sugar will begin to melt and bubble. At this point, lower heat a bit. Do not allow sugar to get very dark brown or burn.

4 Quickly and carefully, add chicken and marinade to bubbly, brown melted sugar.

5 Cover pot for a minute, then uncover again and stir pieces until all are browned in pot. Cover again. Turn back up heat to medium.

6 Turn pieces every now and again, allowing liquid to evaporate partially, but not completely, about 15 minutes. If drying out, add about ½-1 cup of water. Chicken should be cooked until tender, 30 minutes total.

7 During the last 10 minutes of cooking, add tomatoes and bell peppers.

Menu Suggestion Quinoa, Great Green Beans (p. 179) or Cumin Carrots (p. 176), Standby Green salad (p. 74)

Nutrition Snapshot *Per serving: 200 calories, 8g fat, 3g saturated fat, 26g protein, 7g carbs, 3g fiber, 440mg sodium*

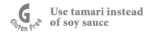
Use tamari instead
of soy sauce

Asian-Style Beef with Cabbage and Mushrooms

Fast, flavorful, and not forbidden! Yes, you can eat beef and feel good about it. Lean beef is not off-limits but is meant to be eaten only 1-2 times per week — unless it's 100-percent grass fed, in which case it can be eaten more frequently. Cabbage, on the other hand, is truly a superfood that many undervalue and eat too infrequently. Here's a super-quick, delicious way to enjoy this cancer-fighting, slimming superfood for lunch or dinner.

4 **Servings**
Total time 8-10 minutes

1 (1-lb) pkg refrigerated Shaved Beef
1 (12-oz) pkg shredded cabbage
1 (10-oz) pkg sliced baby portabellas
2 Tbsp reduced sodium soy sauce
¼ tsp red pepper flakes

1 Heat a large wok over high heat and add the beef. Using a wooden spatula, stir-fry the beef and break it apart, 3-4 minutes. (Can even tear it with your hands before adding to wok.)

2 Add cabbage and stir-fry about 1 minute.

3 Add mushrooms, soy sauce, and red pepper flakes. Stir-fry another 2-3 minutes, until cabbage and mushrooms are just softened but not overcooked. Serve immediately.

Menu Suggestion Great Green Beans (p. 179), frozen Organic Brown Rice and Spinach Salad Nouveau (p. 76).

Nutrition Snapshot
Per serving: 200 calories, 8g fat, 3g saturated fat, 26g protein, 7g carbs, 3g fiber, 440mg sodium

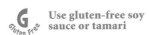

Use gluten-free soy sauce or tamari

Beef Kabobs with Tsatsiki

Kabobs are a lighter way to enjoy beef because the veggies, sauce, and other sides complement it with filling, fabulous flavors that take the focus off the meat. It's a perfect summer meal that doesn't weigh you down like a 16-ounce steak! Kick back, escape to the Mediterranean, and enjoy grilled steak in the right portion.

4 Servings
Total time 30 minutes

Omit tsatsiki
Substitute salsa if desired

1 lb premium steak tips
2 Tbsp olive oil
½ tsp salt
¼ tsp garlic powder

⅛ tsp pepper
3 bell peppers, any color
1 red onion
8 metal or wooden skewers

1 Light the grill or heat a grill pan.

2 Cut steak tips into smaller chunks, golf ball-sized or smaller. Pat dry with a paper towel.

3 Combine oil and seasonings in a bowl and add steak tips. Toss well to coat all pieces.

4 Cut bell peppers and red onion into chunks to match beef size.

5 Make 8 kabobs, alternating beef, onion and pepper and evenly using beef per kabob. (Can also make 4 large kabobs instead.)

6 Grill kabobs over direct heat to desired doneness of beef.

7 Serve immediately with ¼ cup Tsatsiki per serving (see below).

Tsatsiki 4 servings
2 cups (500g container) 2-percent Fage Greek yogurt
½ cup finely diced cucumber
2 Tbsp each chopped fresh chives and parsley
¼ tsp salt

⅛ tsp pepper
1 clove crushed garlic
2 tsp pepper sauce

1 Combine all ingredients. Can make ahead and refrigerate for several hours or overnight.

Menu Suggestion Any of these: Sizzling Spuds with Sage (p. 187), Fly Me to the Moon Arugula Salad (p. 79), Great Greek Salad (p. 86), Light and Lemony Lentils (p. 170), Love Me Lentil Salad (p. 98), Summery Quinoa (p. 169), Minty Fruit Salad (p. 222)

Nutrition Snapshot
Per serving of 2 kabobs with ¼ cup tsatsiki: 310 calories, 12g fat, 3g saturated fat, 37g protein, 13g carbs, 2g fiber, 580mg sodium

Roast Rosemary Pork

Lean, tender pork tenderloin creates a "red meat" meal that is light, fragrant and flavorful. It is a good accompaniment to some simple vegetable sides and even makes for a great summer picnic or outdoor eating.

4 **Servings**
Total time 35 minutes

1 lb pork tenderloin
3 large sprigs fresh rosemary
1 tsp olive oil
Garlic powder
¼ tsp salt
¼ tsp black pepper

1 Preheat oven to 375°F.

2 Place rosemary in a line on baking tray.

3 Remove pork loin from package, rinse with water and pat dry with paper towels.

4 Place pork on bed of rosemary and rub with olive oil just to coat entire surface.

5 Sprinkle pork lightly with garlic powder, salt and fresh ground black pepper.

6 Put on low rack in the oven and cook for 30-35 minutes.

7 Remove from oven, let stand a few minutes before slicing and serving.

Menu Suggestion Any of these: Summer Squash and Grape Tomatoes (p. 180), Light and Lemony Lentils (p. 170), Summery Quinoa (p. 169), Quick and Savory Sautéed Cabbage (p. 175), Minty Fruit Salad (p. 222)

Nutrition Snapshot
Per serving: 130 calories, 5g fat, 1g saturated fat, 23g protein, 0g carbs, 0g fiber, 400mg sodium

Dijon Salmon with Artichokes

It may be hard to believe, but this rich-tasting dish is great for you thanks to "detoxifying" artichokes and lemons combined with good fats from salmon and olive oil. I was thrilled to discover the frozen artichokes at TJ's, and the bag literally spoke to me and told me what to do with them. I think you'll be happy they did!

3 **Servings**
Total time 25 minutes

1 lb fresh salmon fillet
1 Tbsp olive oil
1 white onion, peeled and sliced
1 (10-oz) pkg frozen artichoke hearts (or substitute canned ones)
3 Tbsp Dijon mustard
¼ cup white wine
3 lemons
¼ tsp salt
⅛ tsp black pepper

1 Preheat oven to 375°F.

2 In a large cast iron skillet or oven-safe pan, heat olive oil on medium-high heat.

3 Add onion and cook for 2 minutes, or until softened.

4 Add artichokes, mustard, and white wine.

5 Using a spatula, make room for salmon and place in pan.

6 Slice lemons and squeeze juice over salmon, using a mesh strainer to catch seeds.

7 Toss lemon halves in pan. Cover salmon with artichoke sauce and sprinkle with salt and pepper.

8 Bake uncovered in the oven for 18-20 minutes. Serve immediately.

Menu Suggestion Serve with Melt-In-Your-Mouth Mâche salad (p. 91)

Nutrition Snapshot

Per serving: 130 calories, 5g fat, 1g saturated fat,
23g protein, 0g carbs, 0g fiber, 400mg sodium

Perfect Pan-Fried White Fish (Cod or Tilapia) with Green Chili Sauce

Two words that don't typically go together are perhaps "fried" and "diet." Deep-fat frying — at home or in restaurants — is not a cooking method I ever recommend. You may be surprised and delighted to find out that light pan-frying is one of my favorite cooking methods and is still a healthy way to cook. This recipe is the only one in the book that is floured (not breaded) and "fried." For kids, it's a healthier version of the frozen, breaded fishsticks they love. In my house, this one guarantees empty plates without complaints!

4 **Servings**
Total time 20 minutes

**Omit Green Chili Sauce
Substitute salsa if desired**

4 cod or tilapia fillets
1/3 cup white whole wheat flour
¼ tsp salt
¼ tsp cayenne pepper
¼ tsp garlic powder
1-2 Tbsp olive oil

1　Make Green Chili Sauce (see below).

2　In a large Zip Loc® bag or shallow dish, combine flour with spices.

3　Heat 1 Tbsp oil in a large, heavy frying pan over medium heat.

4　Dredge fish in flour mixture until well-coated and then shake off excess. Place in frying pan.

5　Lightly fry fish on both sides until golden brown and fish is white throughout (not glassy), about 3 minutes per side. Add another 1 Tbsp oil if necessary or frying remaining fillets. Serve immediately with ¼ cup Green Chili Sauce per serving.

Green Chili Sauce
1 (4-oz) can green chilies
1 cup nonfat Greek yogurt
¼ tsp salt
Dash cayenne pepper

1　Combine all ingredients. Can make ahead and refrigerate for several hours or overnight.

Nutrition Snapshot
Per serving: 130 calories, 5g fat, 1g saturated fat, 2
3g protein, 0g carbs, 0g fiber, 400mg sodium

Menu Suggestion

Standby Green Salad (p. 74) and Loaded Black Bean Salad (p. 100) or any of the following: Savory White Beans and Spinach (p. 188), Eggcellent Asparagus (p. 200), Sesame Roasted Broccoli (p. 199), Cumin Carrots (p. 176), Great Green Beans (p. 179) or Summer Squash and Grape Tomatoes (p. 180).

Skillet Shrimp and Quinoa

It doesn't get much healthier than this! But don't even think about that — just savor it because it's so delicious. In case you need to know, however, this is a high-fiber and high-protein combination that offers a winning combination of vitamins, minerals, and phytochemicals.

5 **Servings**
Total time 20 minutes

1 cup uncooked quinoa, rinsed
1 lb Uncooked Wild Blue Shrimp (or other frozen uncooked shrimp)
1 red bell pepper, cored, seeded and chopped
1 cup sliced button mushrooms (or any type you like)
2 cups broccoli florets
2 carrots, peeled and chopped
4 Tbsp olive oil, divided
¼ cup chopped fresh basil
½ tsp salt
¼ tsp pepper
¼ tsp garlic powder

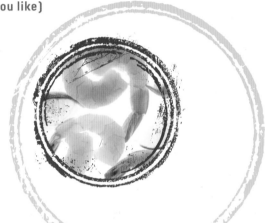

1 Cook quinoa according to instructions. Set aside.

2 Heat 3 Tbsp oil in electric or stovetop skillet.

3 Add broccoli and carrots, cook about 3-4 minutes.

4 Add bell pepper and mushrooms, and cook another 3 minutes.

5 Add shrimp, basil, and seasonings. Cook for about 4-5 minutes.

6 Stir in cooked quinoa. Drizzle with remaining olive oil. Serve immediately.

Note You can use any variety of vegetables you like. For fall, add kohlrabi, turnips, leeks, or even rutabaga, sweet potato, or butternut squash chunks. For great flavor variety, season with combinations of oregano, rosemary, and thyme.

Menu Suggestion Serve with any salad; it's also a complete dish on its own.

Nutrition Snapshot

Per serving: 330 calories, 12g fat, 1g saturated fat, 25g protein, 28g carbs, 5g fiber, 400mg sodium

Salmon with Sunshine Salsa

This broiled salmon is jazzed up with great flavors from a salsa I "doctored up" with fresh tropical fruits and cucumber. It's a summertime favorite, and anytime you see fresh pineapple and mango at TJ's, you can enjoy this dish.

6 **Servings**
Total time 20 minutes

1 ½ lb salmon fillets
1 (12-oz) jar Pineapple Salsa
1 cup chopped fresh pineapple
1 cup chopped fresh mango
1 cup peeled and chopped seedless cucumber (very small chunks)
2 Tbsp each chopped fresh mint and basil
1 lime
1 tsp olive oil
¼ tsp ground cumin (optional)
¼ tsp salt
Pepper to taste

1 Mix together jar of salsa with pineapple, mango, cucumber, and herbs. Squeeze on lime juice. Set aside or make ahead and let chill.

2 Rub salmon with olive oil and sprinkle with cumin, salt, and pepper.

3 Broil salmon 10-12 minutes.

4 Remove from oven, turn onto serving platter and cover with salsa. Serve immediately.

Menu Suggestion Organic Brown Rice or quinoa, Standby Green Salad (p. 74, arugula version recommended)

Nutrition Snapshot
Per serving: 300 calories, 16g fat, 3.5g saturated fat,
24g protein, 16g carbs, 1g fiber, 400mg sodium

Dijon-Dill Rotini with Salmon, Edamame, and Asparagus

This heart-healthy great dish is made easily and inexpensively using frozen veggies and canned salmon. It's an easy way to get your DHA omega-3 as well as potassium, antioxidants, and fiber, and it's an any-time-of-year dish. Of course, it tastes great too.

8 **Servings**
Total time 15 minutes

8 oz rotini pasta
1 (6-oz) can Wild Alaskan Pink Salmon (skinless, boneless, no salt added)
6 oz frozen asparagus spears (or ½ lb fresh)
1 cup frozen shelled edamame
Dijon-Dill Sauce (below)

1 Cook pasta according to instructions.

2 Cut frozen asparagus spears into thirds.

3 After 6 minutes into cooking, add edamame to pasta and cook/boil for another 4 minutes.

4 Add asparagus at the end for less than a minute. Note: If using fresh asparagus, add to cooking water for last 3 minutes.

5 Drain in colander and transfer to a serving bowl. Add canned salmon.

6 Pour on Dijon-Dill Sauce (see below) and mix well to distribute sauce evenly.

Dijon-Dill Sauce
Juice of 3 lemons
1/3 cup olive oil
2 Tbsp Dijon mustard
3 Tbsp chopped fresh dill
¼ tsp salt

1 Whisk together sauce ingredients.

Note Double sauce to add to leftover pasta for lunch the next day.

Menu Suggestion Standby Green Salad (p. 74)

Nutrition Snapshot
Per serving: 260 calories, 13g fat, 1.5g saturated fat, 12g protein, 24g carbs, 4g fiber, 300mg sodium

 Use gluten-free pasta

Spicy Shrimp Spaghetti

This dish is like a pasta puttanesca and arrabiata rolled into one complete meal. If you ask me, it's a perfect combination of flavors and nutrients! Since it's a Mediterranean dish, a side salad and glass of chardonnay round it out perfectly.

8 **Servings**
Total time 25 minutes

10 oz spaghetti
1 lb Uncooked Wild Blue Shrimp (or other frozen uncooked shrimp)
3 Tbsp olive oil
1 shallot, peeled and chopped
3 cloves garlic, peeled and finely chopped, or 2 tsp chopped garlic from a jar
2 (15-oz) cans no added sodium diced tomatoes
1 cup broccoli florets, cut into small pieces
¼ cup pitted, sliced kalamata olives
1 tsp each dried oregano and thyme, or 1 Tbsp fresh chopped
½ tsp crushed red pepper flakes
½ tsp salt
Pepper to taste

1 If using frozen shrimp, place in a colander under running water for about 5 minutes to thaw.

2 Cook spaghetti according to instructions.

3 In a large, deep pan, heat oil over medium heat and add shallot and garlic. Cook until tender, then add tomatoes, broccoli, olives, oregano, thyme, and pepper flakes; cook covered for about 8 minutes.

4 Add shrimp and cook for 5 minutes or only until shrimp are cooked and opaque.

5 Add salt and pepper to taste. Serve immediately.

Note Leftover pasta will keep and reheat very nicely for a several days, and the flavor is even better, but I don't recommend reheating shrimp. (Eat it all and add grilled shrimp or chicken to the leftover spaghetti if you want the extra protein.)

Menu Suggestion Standby Green Salad (p. 74)

Nutrition Snapshot

Per serving: 270 calories, 7g fat, 1g saturated fat, 18g protein, 34g carbs, 4g fiber, 280mg sodium

G Gluten Free **Use gluten-free pasta**

Buffalo Chicken and Asparagus Penne

Decadent but oh-so-good and still pretty darn healthful. Penne pasta, chicken, asparagus, and red peppers come together in a delicious and rich cream sauce. Thank the asparagus for giving it some potassium, folate, and fiber and the red peppers for added vitamin C as well as great flavor.

8 **Servings**
Total time 15 minutes

1 (12-oz) pkg Just Chicken White Meat Chicken
10 oz penne pasta
1 (12-oz) pkg fresh asparagus
1 (5-oz) container Spreadable Bleu Cheese
16 oz low-fat sour cream (nonfat can be used as well)
3 Tbsp chili pepper sauce (more if desired)
½ tsp salt
⅛ tsp pepper
1 (12-oz) jar Fire Roasted Red Peppers, drained and sliced

1 Cook penne according to instructions.

2 Clean asparagus and cut about 1 inch off the stem and discard. Cut the rest into 1-inch pieces.

3 While pasta is cooking, in a medium saucepan combine sour cream, bleu cheese, chili pepper sauce, salt, and pepper. Let cook over low-medium heat until melted and blended.

4 Add asparagus to pasta water about 1 minute before done cooking. Pour into colander to drain then pour into serving bowl.

5 Add red peppers and chicken and then pour cream sauce over it.

6 Combine well and serve immediately. Season with more chili pepper sauce as desired.

Menu Suggestion Standby Green Salad (p. 74)

Nutrition Snapshot

Per serving: 325 calories, 7g fat, 6g saturated fat, 23g protein, 33g carbs, 4g fiber, 450mg sodium

 **Use gluten-free pasta**

"Creamy" Red Pepper-Basil Pasta

Penne with vodka sauce has to be one of my all-time favorite meals and is the inspiration behind this recipe. I just love making this dish for people because they're always amazed when I tell them how I made the creamy sauce. It's a pasta indulgence without an ounce of guilt. It's also a meal that makes the entire family happy! If you're feeding a large family or group, this recipe is easily doubled.

6 **Servings**
Total time 35-40 minutes (including baking)

8 oz penne pasta
½ carton (16 oz) Low-Sodium Organic Tomato and Roasted Red Pepper Soup
1 (12-oz) jar Fire Roasted Red Peppers, drained and cut in small slices
⅓ cup chopped fresh basil
1 ½ cups frozen petite peas
4 oz crème fraîche or light cream cheese
½ tsp salt
¼ tsp black pepper
3 Tbsp grated Parmesan cheese

1 Put pot of water on to boil for pasta and cook according to instructions.

2 Preheat oven to 375°F.

3 While pasta cooks, heat soup, red peppers, basil, and peas in a medium saucepan over medium heat. Stir in crème fraîche, salt, and pepper. Let cook 1-2 minutes.

4 Drain pasta and pour into a shallow baking dish.

5 Pour sauce over pasta and stir to evenly cover pasta.

6 Sprinkle Parmesan cheese on top and bake for 20-25 minutes, until bubbly and slightly browned on top.

Note For added creaminess without any added fat, replace crème fraîche with fat-free cream cheese.

Menu Suggestion Standby Green Salad (p. 74, arugula or spinach recommended)

Nutrition Snapshot
Per 1 cup serving: 230 calories, 3g fat, 1g saturated fat,
9g protein, 40g carbs, 6g fiber, 430mg sodium

   Use gluten-free pasta

Going Green Rotini

This pasta gone green tastes so good that kids love it too. Any veggies can be used, and I let my kids cherry pick which veggies they want. It's one yummy phytonutrient bomb, and if you're looking for a summertime picnic potluck dish, look no further.

8 **Servings**
Total time 15 minutes

10 oz rotini (or pasta of choice)
½ lb asparagus
½ cup sugar snap peas
2 cups broccoli florets
2 lemons
¼ cup olive oil
1 clove garlic, crushed
¼ cup chopped fresh basil
½ tsp salt
¼ tsp pepper
8 Tbsp Parmesan cheese

1 Cook pasta in large pot.

2 Cut tough ends off asparagus (about 1 inch at bottom) and cut spears into thirds.

3 After 5 minutes of cooking pasta, add asparagus, sugar snap peas, and broccoli. Cook 2-3 more minutes, until pasta is soft and vegetables are tender but not overcooked.

4 Pour pasta/veggies into colander to drain, then transfer to serving bowl.

5 Squeeze lemons over a strainer (to catch seeds) into a small bowl. Add olive oil, crushed garlic, basil, salt, and pepper. Stir together and pour over pasta.

6 Add 1 Tbsp grated Parmesan cheese per serving. Toss, serve and savor!

Menu Suggestion Great alone or as accompaniment to Best-Loved Chicken Balsamico (p. 122), Favorite Summer Salad (p. 82)

Nutrition Snapshot

Per serving: 220 calories, 9.5g fat, 2g saturated fat,
9g protein, 28g carbs, 5g fiber, 250mg sodium

 Use gluten-free pasta

Pumpkin-Lentil Penne

When canned pumpkin hits the shelves, this penne dish is a must! You may be shocked to find how delicious this hearty and heart-healthy sauce tastes, and, with vitamins A and C and iron, it may help stave off the winter flu, too.

16 **Servings**
Total time 25 minutes

10 oz penne pasta
2 Tbsp olive oil
2 cloves garlic, peeled and minced
1 (14.5-oz) container Mirepoix (or 1 cup each chopped carrots, onion, and celery)
1 (17.6-oz) pkg refrigerated Steamed Lentils
2 cups low sodium chicken or vegetable broth
1 (15-oz) can pumpkin purée
1 (15-oz) can diced tomatoes
¼ cup chopped fresh basil
2 tsp dried oregano (or 1 Tbsp fresh, chopped)
½ tsp each salt and pepper
¼ cup half and half (optional)
¼ cup water as needed

1 Heat oil in a large saucepan on low-medium heat. Add garlic and Mirepoix and cook for 3-4 minutes, until tender.

2 Add lentils, broth, pumpkin, tomatoes, basil, oregano, salt, and pepper. Cook covered on low heat for 10-15 minutes.

3 Cook pasta according to instructions. Drain and transfer to serving bowl.

4 Add half and half (if desired) and water to sauce if sauce is too thick.

5 Combine pasta and lentil sauce.

Menu Suggestion Standby Green Salad (p. 74)

Nutrition Snapshot
Per 1 cup serving: 150 calories, 2g fat, 0g saturated fat, 6g protein, 27g carbs, 6g fiber, 140mg sodium

 Use vegetable broth
Vegan option: omit
half and half

 Use gluten-free
pasta

Chicken Pesto Pasta with Broccoli and Beans

Fresh basil pesto is one of my favorite things in the world, and when I don't make it myself, the fresh Genova Pesto at TJ's comes in handy. Yes, it's high in fat, but thankfully a little goes a long way in this delicious one-pot combination of filling, high-fiber, nutrient-dense foods. Try it with shrimp instead of chicken, or for a vegetarian version, use pesto-marinated tofu or simply omit chicken. Packed with fiber, protein, vitamins and minerals, it will fill you with great-tasting calories that won't send your blood sugar into orbit!

8 Servings
Total time 20 minutes

8 oz penne or rotini pasta
1 (12-oz) pkg Just Chicken White Meat Chicken
      (or 2 grilled skinless, boneless chicken breasts)
1 Tbsp olive oil
1 (12-oz) pkg broccoli florets
1 (15-oz) can red kidney beans, drained
½ cup refrigerated Genova Pesto
¼ tsp salt
¼ cup grated fresh Parmesan cheese

1   Cook the pasta according to instructions (about 8 minutes). Add broccoli 3 minutes before pasta is finished cooking.

2   Remove pasta from heat and add beans right before draining cooking water (to warm the beans). Then pour into colander to drain and transfer to serving bowl.

3   Add chicken to pasta, broccoli, and beans. Stir in pesto and sprinkle with salt. Toss well to coat. Serve immediately with 1 Tbsp Parmesan cheese per serving.

Menu Suggestion Standby Green Salad (p. 74, arugula or spinach recommended)

Nutrition Snapshot

Per serving: 300 calories, 9g fat, 1g saturated fat, 23g protein, 32g carbs, 6g fiber, 340mg sodium

G Gluten Free   **Use gluten-free pasta**

Susan's Pseudo Spaghetti Carbonara

Spaghetti carbonara is one of my favorite Italian dishes but is traditionally laden with fat and calories. Here's an enlightened version you're sure to love!

8 **Servings**
Total time 20 minutes

8 oz spaghetti
1 red onion, peeled and chopped
2 cloves garlic, peeled and chopped
3 Tbsp olive oil
3 slices Fully Cooked Uncured Bacon, cut into small pieces
    (or 3 slices Applegate Farms cooked ham)
4 oz reduced-fat cream cheese
1 ½ cups frozen peas
1 Tbsp chopped fresh sage
½ tsp dried thyme
½ tsp dried oregano
2 eggs, lightly beaten
¼ cup grated fresh Parmesan cheese
½ tsp salt and fresh ground pepper to taste

1 Cook spaghetti according to instructions and drain.

2 While spaghetti is cooking, prepare the carbonara.

3 Heat olive oil in a large saucepan using medium heat. Add onion and garlic and cook until onions are very tender.

4 Add bacon and cook 3 minutes before adding cream cheese. Stir until cheese is melted.

5 Add frozen peas and herbs and cook just a few minutes until tender.

6 Add hot cooked spaghetti and stir until sauce is evenly distributed. Pour in eggs and toss entire dish over low-medium heat. Season with salt and pepper.

7 Sprinkle with fresh Parmesan cheese and serve immediately.

Notes Herbs can be replaced with 1-2 tsp Herbs de Provence. No egg, no problem. Tastes great without too! Goat cheese or soy cream cheese can replace regular cream cheese.
Veggie version – simply leave out the bacon.

Menu Suggestion Large serving of Standby Green Salad (p. 74)

 Omit bacon

Nutrition Snapshot *Per serving: 240 calories, 11g fat, 3.5g saturated fat, 11g protein, 27g carbs, 4g fiber, 350mg sodium*

 Use gluten-free pasta

We typically view vegetables as side dishes. It's interesting that they are usually thought of as a complement, and not the main event. My feeling is that many side dishes are sometimes so good that they should take the spotlight. This chapter provides all vegetarian recipes to complement many of the entrées, and any of them can also double as a snack, fill in as an appetizer, or be combined together to create the main course.

Broaden your side-dish horizons while lightening up your plate.

Chapter 10
Sides to Slenderize

Quinoa and Brown Rice

These two whole grains can and should be eaten frequently or even daily. (Technically, what we eat is the seed of a fruit named quinoa, but it's not worth splitting hairs on terms when it's used as a grain in the diet.) Start the 2-Week Challenge with both quinoa and brown rice on hand, and try to eat one or the other every day.

If you're not feeling inspired to fix a recipe per se, the easiest way to add these great grains to your meal is by drizzling with olive oil and sprinkling with a dash of salt, then stirring to coat with oil. The addition of the oil brings out quinoa's flavor in particular and adds essential fats. Making these whole grains a part of your regular diet will help with weight management — as opposed to what most people think about grains.

Nutrition Snapshot

Per ½ cup cooked quinoa with 1 tsp olive oil: 150 calories, 6g fat, 0.5g saturated fat, 4g protein, 20g carbs, 3g fiber, 0mg sodium

Per ½ cup frozen Organic Brown Rice with 1 tsp olive oil: 120 calories, 5g fat, 0.5g saturated fat, 2g protein, 17g carbs, 1g fiber, 0mg sodium

Vegetarian G Gluten Free

Summery Quinoa

If you've never tried quinoa, this is the dish I use to get people turned on to it. There's so much goodness in this quick, light, and savory side dish. Quinoa is a complete protein, like eggs and meat, but also gives you the added benefits of fiber, complex carbs, and lots of minerals, including iron, calcium, potassium, magnesium, and zinc. No wonder this ancient grain has staying power!

6 **Servings**
Total time 15 minutes

1 cup uncooked quinoa
½ cup shelled edamame (fresh or frozen)
1 ½ cups chopped carrots (about 2 carrots)
1 cup chopped red bell pepper
¼ cup fresh mint, chopped
1 large lemon
3 Tbsp olive oil
½ tsp salt

1 Rinse quinoa with cold water and cook quinoa according to instructions (12 minutes cooking once water boils). When done, transfer to serving bowl.

2 If using frozen edamame, microwave it for 1½ minutes on high power to thaw.

3 Add all vegetables and mint to quinoa and toss.

4 Squeeze lemon over quinoa using a small strainer to catch seeds.

5 Pour on olive oil, add salt, and toss well. Serve and enjoy!

Nutrition Snapshot

Per 1 cup serving: 250 calories, 10g fat, 1g saturated fat, 7g protein, 33g carbs, 5g fiber, 220mg sodium

Light and Lemony Lentils

Here is a must-eat item on the 2-Week Challenge and beyond, thanks to the detoxifying combination of lemons, parsley, and artichokes. You'll love how easy, flavorful, and filling this perfect side dish is. It goes well with pork loin, salmon, chicken, or simply served with other sides such as a quinoa salad or brown rice to make a great vegetarian meal.

8 **Servings**
Total time 10 minutes

1 (17.6-oz) pkg refrigerated Steamed Lentils
4 Whole Artichokes with Stems, drained
½ lb asparagus
2 lemons for juice and zest
2 Tbsp olive oil
¼ cup chopped fresh parsley
½ tsp salt
Pepper to taste

1   Put lentils in a glass bowl.

2   Slice stems off artichokes, then slice in quarters. Add to lentils.

3   Slice 1 inch off the bottoms of asparagus. Place in a shallow pan and add ¼ cup water.

4   Place pan with asparagus on stove over high heat and bring to a boil. Allow to cook/steam for just 2 minutes. Remove immediately and rinse with cold water.

5   Cut asparagus into smaller pieces and add to lentils.

6   Zest lemons over lentils, then slice in half and squeeze juice onto lentils, using a mesh strainer to catch seeds.

7   Add parsley, salt, and pepper. Combine well. Serve immediately or refrigerate for several hours.

Nutrition Snapshot

Per serving: 130 calories, 3g fat, 0g saturated fat, 7g protein, 17g carbs, 7g fiber, 320mg sodium

Bold and Beautiful Brussels Sprouts

It took until adulthood for me to give Brussels sprouts a chance, and now I even look forward to these little cruciferous vegetables formerly known as "gag balls." Glad I got over my aversion, because Brussels sprouts are loaded with cancer-fighting phytochemicals. I made this dish after having a version like it with red grapes in a restaurant — it tasted like candy! (And I know my dish has far less salt and oil!)

4 **Servings**
Total time 10 minutes

1 (16-oz) pkg Brussels sprouts, sliced in half
2 Tbsp olive oil
½ cup sliced seedless red grapes
¼ cup balsamic vinegar
¼ tsp salt

1 Add olive oil to a large skillet and heat over medium-high heat.

2 Add sprouts and cook for several minutes, letting some individual leaves fall off and start to get browned.

3 Add grapes, balsamic vinegar, and salt; cook and stir for 3 minutes.

4 Cover and let cook another 2 minutes. Remove lid, let cook 1 minute, and serve immediately.

Nutrition Snapshot

*Per serving: 140 calories, 7g fat, 1g saturated fat,
4g protein, 18g carbs, 4g fiber, 170mg sodium*

Vegetarian G Gluten Free

Quick and Savory Sautéed Cabbage

The lowly little cabbage rarely takes the spotlight on the plate, but this cruciferous vegetable is known to be one of the most powerful when it comes to disease and fat-fighting. It is loaded with phytochemicals which ward off cancer, and cabbage has long been used for its weight-loss support, since it is very low in calories yet nutrient-dense. When it comes to nutritional value per dollar, cabbage is the ultimate trophy winner!

4 **Servings**
Total time 5 minutes

1 (10-oz) pkg shredded cabbage
2 Tbsp canola oil
2 Tbsp rice vinegar
½ tsp dried thyme
¼ tsp salt
Pepper to taste

1 Heat oil in a wok on medium-high heat. Add the cabbage and stir-fry for 1 minute.

2 Add vinegar, thyme, and seasonings. Stir-fry another 2-3 minutes until tender.

Nutrition Snapshot

Per serving: 80 calories, 7g fat, 0.5g saturated fat,
1g protein, 4g carbs, 2g fiber, 170mg sodium

Cumin Carrots

Over the years, cooked carrots have gotten a bad reputation for being a high-glycemic index food. In reality, carrots have a very low glycemic load and are a low-calorie, low-carb, nutrient-dense food. They are loaded with cancer-preventing phytochemicals, and when cooked slightly, these compounds become more readily available. Adding a little oil helps the body absorb all that great vitamin A, a fat-soluble vitamin. Bottom line: Munch on them any time. These carrots pair up nicely with Pan-Fried Tilapia (p. 142) and Chicken Balsamico (p. 122).

4 **Servings**
Total time 10 minutes

1 lb (about 8) carrots, peeled, or 1 bag baby carrots
¼ cup water
1 Tbsp olive oil
½ tsp cumin
¼ tsp garlic powder
½ tsp red pepper flakes
½ tsp salt
Pepper to taste
1 Tbsp orange juice or 1 tsp orange juice concentrate

1 Slice carrots into strips, about 4 inches long and ¼-inch wide.

2 Heat water in a medium-sized frying pan till bubbling and add carrots. Let cook/steam for 2 minutes.

3 Add oil and seasonings. Stir and let cook another 2 minutes.

4 Toss with orange juice and serve immediately.

Nutrition Snapshot

Per serving: 80 calories, 4g fat, 0.5g saturated fat, 1g protein, 11g carbs, 3g fiber, 220mg sodium

Great Green Beans

Green beans are a common vegetable that kids seem to like, but they aren't a nutrition commoner. They are high in folate and other vitamins, fiber, and phytochemicals, and they're not a vegetable that people tend to dislike! In other words — serve them often, and they will be eaten.

4 **Servings**
Total time 15 minutes

1 lb fresh or frozen green beans (or haricot verts)
2 Tbsp olive oil
2 cloves garlic, peeled and chopped
2 cups chopped celery (2 or 3 stalks)
½ tsp salt
⅛ tsp pepper

1 Heat olive oil in a large pan over medium heat and add garlic. Cook 1 minute, making sure garlic does not get browned.

2 Add celery and stir around pan to cook about 1 or 2 minutes.

3 Add green beans, salt, and pepper, stir and then cover. Let cook 6-7 minutes.

Nutrition Snapshot

Per serving: 100 calories, 7g fat, 1g saturated fat,
2g protein, 9g carbs, 4g fiber, 320mg sodium

Summer Squash and Grape Tomatoes

I have to confess, I like to serve this dish on the side of homemade mac 'n' cheese (which is really whole grain bowties 'n' cheese in my house). This healthy and tasty combination livens up the plate and the palate — definitely a reason to love simple summer foods!

4 **Servings**
Total time 10 minutes

2 zucchini or summer squash
¼ tsp salt
¼ cup water
1 Tbsp olive oil
1 ½ cups grape tomatoes
2 or 3 cloves garlic, chopped
¼ tsp dried thyme
¼ tsp dried oregano
¼ tsp salt

1   Slice squash into ¼ inch thick rounds.

2   Pour water in pan and add squash and ¼ tsp salt.

3   Bring water to boil, cover, and steam squash 3 minutes.

4   Uncover and add oil, tomatoes, garlic, herbs, and salt.

5   Toss and stir vegetables around in pan until herbs, oil, and garlic look evenly distributed while cooking, about 2 minutes.

6   Cover and let cook 2 minutes. Serve immediately.

Note If using fresh herbs instead of dried, use 1 Tbsp of each

Nutrition Snapshot
Per serving: 55 calories, 4g fat, 0.5g saturated fat,
1g protein, 5g carbs, 1g fiber, 300mg sodium

Eggplant-Artichoke Wraps

These can serve as an appetizer as well as side dish. I keep the skin on the eggplant because that's where the antioxidants are found, and it helps hold the fleshy eggplant together when you grill it.

6 **Servings**
Total time 20-25 minutes

1 eggplant
Olive oil (or spray oil)
1 (14.6-oz) jar Whole Artichokes with Stems
3 oz Lite Celtic Cheddar cheese
Basil
Salt
Pepper
Lemon juice

1 Preheat oven to 375°F. Slice eggplant thinly and sprinkle with salt and let sit 3-5 minutes. Pat dry with paper towel before grilling.

2 Rub bottom of a large grill pan with olive oil. Heat grill pan using medium-high heat, then place slices of eggplant in pan. (Only a few will fit at a time.)

3 Grind or just sprinkle a dash of salt over eggplant and grill for 3-4 minutes, or until soft and has nice brown grill marks. Flip and grill another 2 minutes.

4 Place eggplant on baking dish. Slice artichokes in half and place one half on each eggplant slice.

5 Grate about 1 Tbsp cheese onto each artichoke. Top with a small piece of basil and then dash of salt and pepper. Fold each eggplant to cover artichokes.

6 Bake for 10 minutes and serve immediately.

Nutrition Snapshot

Two wraps per serving: 80 calories, 2g fat, 1g saturated fat, 6g protein, 9g carbs, 4g fiber, 250mg sodium

Sweet Potato and Black Bean Fritters

This side dish can double as a satisfying vegetarian main course, particularly when served with a side of Brussels sprouts and a salad. That's a perfect meal to me, both nutritionally and gastronomically!

Makes 10 fritters
Total time 30 minutes

1 ½ lb (about 4 large) sweet potatoes
2 shallots
2 Tbsp olive oil
1 (15-oz) can black beans, rinsed and drained
3 Tbsp chopped fresh rosemary
1 egg
½ cup bread crumbs
¼ tsp salt
Olive oil spray
Goat cheese to serve (optional)

1 Rinse potatoes, poke them with knife, and microwave on high for 6 minutes or until softened but not mushy.

2 In a large frying pan, heat oil on medium heat and add shallots. Cook 2 minutes, until tender.

3 Add beans and rosemary, and let sit on low heat.

4 Peel potatoes, cut in chunks, and add to beans and shallots. Stir and cook over medium heat another 2-3 minutes. Remove from heat, and put mixture in a large mixing bowl.

5 Add egg, bread crumbs, and salt to sweet potatoes. Using hands or a wooden spoon, combine well to fully incorporate bread crumbs and egg.

6 Heat the same frying pan again over medium heat, and spray with cooking spray.

7 Using your hands, form slightly smaller than palm-sized fritters and place in frying pan. Fry each one 4-5 minutes per side or until browned and look slightly crispy. Serve immediately with crumbled goat cheese on top

Nutrition Snapshot

Per fritter: 120 calories, 3g fat, 1g saturated fat,
3g protein, 21g carbs, 2g fiber, 140mg sodium

Sizzling Spuds with Sage

When you hear these potatoes cooking in the oven, you know how they got their name. It's a happy sound and a smart way to cook and enjoy a small amount of our beloved spuds—full of potassium, fiber, and complex carbs.

4 **Servings**
Total time 30 minutes

1 (16-oz) bag Fingerling Potatoes
2 Tbsp olive oil
3 Tbsp chopped fresh sage
¼ tsp salt

1 Preheat oven to 425°F.

2 Toss potatoes in a bowl with oil, sage, and salt.

3 Pour into baking dish and bake in oven for 25 minutes. Serve immediately.

Nutrition Snapshot

Per serving: 170 calories, 7g fat, 1g saturated fat,
3g protein, 24g carbs, 3g fiber, 160mg sodium

Vegetarian Gluten Free

Savory White Beans and Spinach

The quantity of spinach in this recipe would make Popeye proud, and the amount of fiber will keep the doctor away! This dish is not only good for your muscles, it's loaded with nutrients that are good for your eyes, immune and digestive systems, and especially your heart. It's hard to find a more delicious way to get your daily fiber than from greens, beans, and garlic. With nearly half your day's fiber requirement, this dish fills you up with all the right stuff.

6 **Servings**
Total time 10 minutes

2 (15-oz) cans white kidney beans, rinsed
2 Tbsp olive oil
3 cloves garlic, chopped
3 (6-oz) bags fresh spinach or 1 (16-oz) bag frozen spinach
¼ cup broth or water
¼ tsp red pepper flakes
½ tsp salt
Pepper to taste

1 Heat oil in a large pan on medium heat. Add garlic and let cook 1 minutes.

2 Add spinach to pan and stir, cooking spinach down for 1-2 minutes.

3 Add broth or water, beans, and seasonings.

4 Stir gently and let cook another 3 minutes.

5 Season to taste with more pepper or pepper flakes and serve immediately.

Nutrition Snapshot

Per serving: 200 calories, 5g fat, 0.5g saturated fat,
11g protein, 28g carbs, 13g fiber, 500mg sodium

  Choose gluten-free broth

Although a great kick-off to entertaining, appetizers often include double or triple the calories of the meal that follows. Recipes in this chapter will help you impress friends without contributing to their "battle of the bulge "

Chapter 11

Easy Appetizers

Romaine Leaves with Langostino Salad

Langostino salad served on romaine leaves is a must-have at your next party or get together. You can make the "little lobster" salad ahead of time and refrigerate for several hours or overnight. The mayonnaise coating ends up being very subtle and light, and the overall result is a guilt-free appetizer you'll love and love serving to guests.

16 **Servings**
Total time 15 minutes (excluding refrigeration)

1 (8-oz) pkg frozen langostino tails, thawed
½ cup frozen roasted corn, thawed
1 lemon
¼ cup chopped fresh parsley
2 Tbsp chopped fresh chives
1 Tbsp Wasabi Mayo
1 Tbsp mayonnaise
¼ tsp salt
Pepper to taste
1 head Romaine lettuce hearts

1 Combine langostino tails and corn in a bowl and squeeze lemon over them, using a mesh strainer to catch seeds.

2 Add herbs, both mayos, salt, and pepper. Stir to combine well. Cover and refrigerate for at least 30 minutes before serving.

3 Cut each lettuce piece into 2 or 3 pieces and scoop 1 Tbsp langostino salad onto each Romaine lettuce wedge.

Nutrition Snapshot
Per salad wedge: 40 calories, 1.5g fat, 0.5g saturated fat, 4g protein, 2g carbs, 0.5g fiber, 110mg sodium

Polenta, Pesto, Beet, and Basil Bites

These lovely polenta appetizers are a color and flavor explosion! Instead of puff pastry or crackers, use polenta and beets, adding interest and nutritional value to your party table.

16 **Servings**
Total time 20 minutes

1 (18-oz) tube pre-cooked Organic Polenta
Olive oil cooking spray
1 (8-oz) pkg refrigerated Steamed Beets
2 oz goat cheese
¼ cup refrigerated Genova Pesto
6 fresh basil leaves

1 Preheat oven to 400°F. Slice polenta into 18 thin rounds.

2 Spray a frying pan with olive oil cooking spray and heat pan over medium heat. Add polenta rounds (may need to do two or more batches.) Pan-fry on each side until golden brown, about 3-4 minutes per side.

3 Place fried polenta rounds on a baking sheet. Slice beets and place 1 slice on each polenta round.

4 Top with about 1 tsp of goat cheese and ½ tsp pesto per polenta round.

5 Bake for about 10 minutes, remove from oven, and transfer rounds to serving plate.

6 Top each round with small piece fresh basil and serve immediately.

Nutrition Snapshot
Per 1 polenta round: 50 calories, 2g fat, 0.5g saturated fat,
1.5g protein, 6g carbs, 1g fiber, 110mg sodium

Mini Whole Wheat Shroom-Stuffed Pita Pockets

If you told guests that the appetizers they were about to eat were low fat and high fiber, they might graciously say "no thanks." So don't spill the beans until they ask for the recipe, because these are deceptively good.

Makes 16 mini pitas
Total time 10 minutes

16 mini whole wheat pitas
2 cups sliced mushrooms (baby bellas or button)
½ red onion, peeled and finely diced
2 Tbsp olive oil
1 cup fat-free refried beans
2 Tbsp chopped fresh thyme
¼ tsp salt

1 Heat olive oil in a pan over medium heat. Add mushrooms and onion.

2 Let cook about 4-5 minutes before adding beans, thyme, and salt.

3 Stuff each mini-pita with about 1 Tbsp bean mixture. Serve immediately at room temperature.

Suggested Twist Make with TJ's steamed lentils or simply red kidney beans. Add chopped asparagus to mushrooms if desired. Add a bit of crumbled goat or feta cheese if desired.

Nutrition Snapshot
Per stuffed mini-pita: 55 calories, 2g fat, 0g saturated fat,
2g protein, 7g carbs, 2g fiber, 130mg sodium

Sesame Roasted Broccoli

If you're looking to replace the same old raw crudité veggies, this appetizer makes a great scoop for hummus or my roasted red pepper dip. Call me strange, but I love snacking on this beloved broccoli and hope you do too!

6 **Servings**
Total time 15 minutes

1 (12-oz) pkg broccoli florets
1 Tbsp olive oil
1 Tbsp sesame oil
¼ tsp salt
¼ tsp garlic powder

1 Toss broccoli together with oil and seasonings in a bowl.

2 Heat oven to 400°F, spread broccoli onto baking tray and bake for 12 minutes.

3 After roughly 6 minutes, use a spatula to stir broccoli around.

Nutrition Snapshot

Per 2 oz serving: 60 calories, 4.5g fat, 0g saturated fat,
2g protein, 3g carbs, 1g fiber, 110mg sodium

Eggcellent Asparagus

For a small dinner party or luncheon, try this balsamic-spiked asparagus dish for starters. It also makes a great tapas dish. I love making lots of little plates and trying everything!!

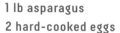

6 Servings
Total time 15 minutes

 **Omit sugar**

1 lb asparagus
2 hard-cooked eggs

1 Slice about 1 inch off the bottoms of asparagus.

2 Place in a medium-sized shallow pan and add about ¼ cup water.

3 Place pan with asparagus on stove over high heat and bring to a boil. Allow to cook/steam for just 2 minutes. Remove immediately and rinse with cold water.

4 Line asparagus on serving plate and grate eggs over it.

5 Drizzle Balsamic Vinaigrette (see below) over eggs and asparagus and serve.

Balsamic Vinaigrette:
1/3 cup balsamic vinegar
1/3 cup olive oil
1-2 cloves garlic, peeled
1 Tbsp Dijon mustard
¼ tsp sugar *(omit during 2-Week Challenge)*
1 pinch salt

1 Whisk together vinaigrette ingredients

Nutrition Snapshot
Per serving: 110 calories, 10g fat, 2g saturated fat,
3g protein, 3g carbs, 1g fiber, 100mg sodium

Red Pepper, Goat Cheese, and Bean Dip

This colorful dip will keep guests guessing what's in it! They also won't believe how good-for-you a great-tasting dip/spread can be.

16 **Servings**
Total time 5 minutes

1 (15-oz) can white kidney beans (cannellini), rinsed and drained
1 (12-oz) jar Fire-Roasted Red Peppers, drained
3 oz goat cheese
1 clove garlic
5 or 6 basil leaves
Dash cayenne pepper (optional)
½ tsp salt

1   Combine all ingredients in a blender and blend until smooth. Serve with cut vegetables and whole wheat pita crackers and/or other crackers.

Nutrition Snapshot

Per 2 Tbsp serving: 40 calories, 1g fat, 0.5g saturated fat,
3g protein, 5g carbs, 2g fiber, 160mg sodium

Spicy Roasted Trail Mix

Addiction warning! This spiced trail mix is simply that good, so be sure to share...

16 **Servings**
Total time 25 minutes

1 (16-oz) bag Simply Cranberry, Cashews, and Almonds trail mix
2 Tbsp olive oil
1 Tbsp sugar
½ tsp cayenne pepper
1 Tbsp chopped fresh rosemary
¼ tsp garlic powder
¼ tsp salt

1 Preheat oven to 375°F.

2 Toss all ingredients together with trail mix in a mixing bowl.

3 Spread evenly onto baking sheet and bake in oven for 20 minutes. After 10 minutes of cooking, remove from oven to stir around on baking sheet and return to oven.

4 Let cool completely before serving. Store in an airtight container for up to 2 weeks.

Nutrition Snapshot

Per 1 oz serving: 160 calories, 10g fat, 1g saturated fat,
5g protein, 13g carbs, 2g fiber, 50mg sodium

It *is* possible to "do" dessert without sabotaging a diet and suffering for a week from guilt. "Just do it, you know you want to!" is the motto for this chapter. If you've worked hard to take the weight off, you'll be happy to know that it really is possible to do dessert without sabotaging your diet success. By choosing right-sized desserts, you can satisfy the desire to indulge your sweet tooth without overdoing it on the calories. This chapter offers some simple yet seemingly decadent desserts to nicely complement a healthy meal or to have as a late afternoon treat. So go ahead, satisfy your sweet tooth guilt-free.

Chapter 12

Doable Desserts

Strawberry Shortcake

Nothing says summer more than strawberry shortcake. I grew up with this summertime treat, and it remains one of my favorites to this day. The smell of biscuits in the oven brings back memories of lazy summer evenings enjoying my mom's homemade shortcake with my family. I've adapted Mom's biscuits to make them multigrain, and the result is a biscuit so simple and so good that you won't miss traditional buttermilk biscuits. Any milk can be used, but I typically use TJ's unsweetened soy milk. Savoring tip: You may want to replenish the mashed strawberries before finishing the biscuit - that's the best way to get strawberry-soaked shortcake in every bite!

Makes 8 biscuits
Total time 25 minutes

2 cups Multigrain Baking & Pancake Mix

2 Tbsp sugar, divided

2/3 cup unsweetened soy milk

3 Tbsp canola oil

Zest of 2 lemons

1 tsp vanilla extract

White whole wheat flour

1 egg, beaten

6 cups strawberries, rinsed and stems removed

Light sweetened whipped cream (in canister)

Fresh mint to garnish

1   Preheat oven to 425°F.

2   Combine multigrain baking mix, 1 Tbsp sugar, soy milk, oil, lemon zest, and vanilla in a bowl until moistened.

3   Turn dough out onto a floured surface and knead it about 10 times. Pat dough down until ½-inch thick and cut with a 2 ½-inch floured biscuit cutter, or simply form biscuits with your hands. (You may need to add flour as you work with the dough.)

4   Place biscuits on ungreased baking sheet and brush top of each with a little egg wash (1 beaten egg). Bake for 8-10 minutes, until golden brown. Let cool completely before using.

5   Reserving about 1 cup whole strawberries, cut the rest in half and place in deep bowl.

6   Add remaining 1 Tbsp sugar and then crush berries with a potato masher to form a juicy, chunky strawberry mix.

7   Slice biscuits in half and spoon about ¼ cup mashed berries over bottom half. Add 4 Tbsp whipped cream and top with other biscuit half. Top with a small amount of cream, 1 fresh strawberry, and sprig of fresh mint.

Nutrition Snapshot

Per serving: 250 calories, 11g fat, 3g saturated fat, 6g protein, 35g carbs, 4g fiber, 400mg sodium

Lemon Blueberry Yogurt Pie

Lemons and blueberries are a match made in heaven, creating a palate-pleasing result. You can feel good about all the berries you're getting if you need to justify this sweet indulgence. For non-bakers, this recipe is about as easy as pie-baking gets, and you're sure to impress family and friends with virtually no effort.

8 **Servings**
Total time 35 minutes

1 frozen pie crust, thawed
1 ½ cups Greek yogurt, non-fat or 2-percent
4 Tbsp Lemon Curd
1 ½ (12-oz) bags frozen wild blueberries, thawed

1 Preheat oven to 400°F.

2 Place crust in 9-inch pie pan according to instructions and bake crust 6 minutes.

3 While crust is pre-baking, stir together yogurt, blueberries and lemon curd in a bowl until well blended.

4 Spoon berry mixture into crust and bake for 25 minutes (until crust is browned and filling starts to crack).

5 Let cool completely before serving.

Nutrition Snapshot
Per serving: 295 calories, 14g fat, 8g saturated fat, 6g protein,37g carbs, 5g fiber, 65mg sodium

Caramel Apple Oat Bars

These crumbly and scrumptious oat bars are so delicious, you'll forget they're made with whole grains, fruit, and nuts. A touch of Fleur de Sel Caramel Sauce adds an irresistible sweet-salty flavor that goes perfectly with apples and cinnamon. These make a crowd-pleasing dessert for entertaining or simply to share with friends over afternoon coffee or a cup of tea.

Makes 16 bars
Total time 1 hour

1 ½ cups white whole wheat flour
½ cup firmly packed organic brown sugar
⅛ tsp salt
1 tsp cinnamon
1 stick (½ cup or 8 Tbsp) unsalted butter

2/3 cup old-fashioned rolled oats
2/3 cup pecans, finely chopped
2 or 3 large apples, peeled
1 lemon
3 Tbsp Fleur de Sel Caramel Sauce

1   Preheat oven to 350°F.

2   Line a 8 x 8-inch baking dish with aluminum foil, making sure it comes up over the sides.

3   In a large bowl, combine flour, sugar, salt, and cinnamon.

4   Cut in the butter into small chunks. Using a pastry cutter or your hands, mix in the butter until the dough becomes crumbly. Stir in oats and pecans to form crumbly dough mixture.

5   Set aside ⅓ of the dough and then transfer remaining ⅔ of the dough into lined baking dish. Press dough firmly into dish to cover bottom evenly.

6   Bake for 20 minutes, until golden brown.

7   Meanwhile, chop apples and place in a bowl.

8   Slice lemon and squeeze juice over apples using a mesh strainer to catch seeds.

9   Add caramel sauce and mix well until apples are evenly coated.

10   Pour apples onto baked crust and press down slightly to make an even layer.

11   Spoon remaining ⅓ dough on apples to make crumb topping.

12   Bake for 25 minutes, or until topping is golden brown. Remove to cooling rack and cool completely before serving.

Nutrition Snapshot

Per 1/16 th serving: 180 calories, 10g fat, 4g saturated fat,
3g protein, 21g carbs, 2g fiber, 50mg sodium

Peach Crisp

Out of all the possible fruit crisp combinations, peach and cinnamon is my favorite, probably because it was my dad's favorite, too. We would go peach-picking and then wait for my mom to turn some into a crisp or pie, and the result with those fresh-from-the-farm delectable peaches was always to die for. No matter how you fill them, fruit crisps are quick, easy and delicious. It's fun to switch up the fruit depending on what's in season, although frozen fruits always work well too.

4 **Servings**
Total time 40 minutes

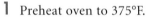

4 peaches, peeled and cut into small pieces
2 Tbsp plus ¼ cup (packed) golden brown sugar
1 tsp ground cinnamon
½ cup old-fashioned rolled oats
2 Tbsp white whole wheat flour
¼ cup ground flax seeds
¼ tsp salt
2 Tbsp (¼ stick) chilled, unsalted butter, cut into small pieces
¼ cup sliced almonds
Light Sweetened Whipped Cream (in canister, optional)

1 Preheat oven to 375°F.

2 Place peaches in 9-inch glass pie dish.

3 Sprinkle with 2 Tbsp brown sugar and cinnamon; stir to blend. Let stand until sugar dissolves and coats peaches.

4 Stir oats, flour, flax, salt, and remaining ¼ cup brown sugar to blend in medium bowl.

5 Add butter and cut in with fingertips or pastry fork until moist clumps form.

6 Stir in almonds.

7 Sprinkle oat mixture evenly over peaches.

8 Bake crisp until fruit is bubbling and topping is golden, about 35 minutes.

9 Serve warm. Can top each serving with 2 Tbsp Light Sweetened Whipped Cream or a spoonful of vanilla frozen yogurt.

Nutrition Snapshot

Per serving: 280 calories, 13g fat, 4g saturated fat,
8g protein, 38g carbs, 7g fiber, 150mg sodium

A Note About Peaches

There's a little negative to peaches now — they're the produce most heavily loaded with pesticides, so I recommend buying organic or at least washing and peeling if conventionally grown. Either way, summer isn't summer without a perfect peach crisp! For summertime breakfasts, chopped fresh peaches sweeten your morning shredded wheat with cinnamon and muesli and pancakes too!

Blend It, Baby Frozen Yogurt

Super-fast, super-easy, super-thick-and-creamy good! It honestly doesn't get easier or faster than this duo that makes a delicious and healthy dessert or snack any time of year. It's not quite a smoothie and not quite a frozen treat, since it is meant to be consumed immediately

2 **Servings**
Total time 3 minutes

1 cup *frozen* mango chunks (or other frozen fruit, such as strawberries, blueberries or banana)

6 oz vanilla yogurt

Fresh mint and strawberries (optional)

1   Pour mango and yogurt into a blender and blend until smooth.

2   Pour into a bowl, top with fresh mint and a strawberry. Serve immediately.

Nutrition Snapshot
Per serving: 140 calories, 0g fat, 0g saturated fat,
4g protein, 30g carbs, 2g fiber, 60mg sodium

Double Nut Chocolate Biscotti

My philosophy on dessert is that if it's got chocolate, it needs a little nuttiness too. The good thing about biscotti is that you can combine a wide variety of ingredients - nuts, extracts, flours, spices, dried fruit - and you still come out with a healthful, low calorie cookie. The chocolate chips give them a little added chocolate boost and sweetness.

Makes 3 dozen biscotti
Total time 1 hour 10 minutes

1 ¾ cups white whole wheat flour
⅓ cup cocoa
½ tsp each baking powder and baking soda
¼ tsp salt
⅛ tsp cinnamon
3 large eggs
¾ cup sugar
1 tsp vanilla extract (almond extract can be used instead)
¼ cup coffee at room temperature
½ cup finely chopped almonds
⅓ cup pecan pieces
½ cup semi-sweet chocolate chips

1 Preheat oven to 300°F. Line baking sheet with parchment paper or grease and flour.

2 In a large bowl, combine flour, cocoa, baking powder, baking soda, salt, and cinnamon; stir until well-blended.

3 In a smaller bowl, beat eggs, sugar, and vanilla together until smooth.

4 Combine egg mixture with flour. Pour in coffee and add nuts and chocolate chips; mix thoroughly to form dough.

5 Using your hands, split dough into two equal parts. Form 2 long strips, each about 13 inches long and 2 ½ inches wide and place on baking sheet about 3 inches apart. With wet fingers, smooth tops and sides.

6 Bake 40 minutes or until firm to the touch. Remove from oven to cooling rack for 5 minutes and reduce oven temp to 275°F.

7 Cut each strip on the diagonal into ½-inch slices. Stand slices on baking sheet about ½ inch apart and bake another 20 minutes. Cool completely before serving.

Nutrition Snapshot *Per biscotti: 70 calories, 3g fat, 1g saturated fat, 2g protein, 11g carbs, 1g fiber, 50mg sodium*

Cranberry Oatmeal Cookies

Cookies are fun to bake, eat, and share with friends. They don't have to be off-limits, especially when loaded with good-for-you ingredients such as cranberries and whole oats. My oatmeal cookies always put a smile on my dad's face at the mere mention of them. These gems are good for your heart and soul, and they're simply irresistible!

Makes 4 dozen cookies
Total time 1 hour

2 sticks (1 cup) butter or margarine (such as Earth Balance)
1 cup packed brown sugar
½ cup sugar
2 eggs
1 ½ tsp vanilla
1 ½ cups white whole wheat flour
1 tsp baking soda
2 tsp cinnamon
¼ tsp salt
3 ½ cups old-fashioned rolled oats
½ (12-oz) bag frozen Sliced Sweetened Cranberries, rinsed

1 Preheat oven to 350°F.

2 Combine flour, soda, cinnamon, and salt and set aside.

3 Cream together butter and sugars until light and fluffy.

4 Add eggs and vanilla and beat well.

5 Add flour mixture and stir until well-blended. Add oats and cranberries and mix well.

6 Spoon heaping teaspoonfuls of batter onto ungreased baking tray or parchment paper on tray and bake 11 minutes or until golden brown.

7 Cool on wire rack before munching. Enjoy!

Note Make these with fresh cranberries when available. Rinsing frozen cranberries removes some added sugar.

Nutrition Snapshot

Per cookie: 95 calories, 5g fat, 3g saturated fat, 2g protein, 12g carbs, 1g fiber, 40mg sodium

Minty Fruit Salad

Fruit makes a perfect energy-boosting, low-calorie snack or dessert, so treat yourself to this vitamin bomb and feel good about it. As a bonus, mint can freshen your breath after a meal

4 Servings
Total time 5 minutes

1 cup sliced strawberries
1 cup blackberries (or blueberries)
2 cups cantaloupe chunks
1 Tbsp chopped fresh mint
1 Tbsp sugar
1 lemon
Light Sweetened Whipped Cream (in canister, optional)

1 Combine all fruit in a large bowl.

2 Sprinkle sugar and mint over fruit and squeeze on juice of lemon using a strainer to catch seeds.

3 Toss together until evenly mixed. Serve immediately or refrigerate for several hours.

4 Serve with 2 Tbsp whipped cream per serving if desired.

Nutrition Snapshot

Per serving: 90 calories, 0.5g fat, 0g saturated fat, 2g protein, 21g carbs, 4g fiber, 20mg sodium
2 Tbsp whipped cream adds 15 calories, 2g fat, 1.5g saturated fat

Vegetarian   Gluten Free

Tropical Delight

It used to be virtually impossible to find tropical fruits in supermarkets, but thankfully they are now more readily available. If you'd rather be in the tropics but can't, at least you can eat as if you are! The inviting colors, natural sweetness, and weight-control benefits of such a vitamin-rich fruit dessert make this a keeper that can be eaten daily if you like. Trader Joe's often has peeled and sliced fresh tropical fruits, cutting the Total time down to nearly nothing.

6 Servings
Total time 5 minutes

2 cups chopped fresh pineapple
2 cups chopped fresh mango
2 cups chopped fresh papaya
2 Tbsp honey
½ tsp cinnamon
1 lime
Crème fraîche (optional)

1 Combine all fruit in a large bowl.

2 Slice lime in half and squeeze juice into a microwavable dish or glass measuring cup.

3 Add honey and cinnamon and microwave on high for about 25 seconds. Pour over fruit.

4 Toss until fruit is evenly coated with honey-lime-cinnamon syrup.

5 Serve in individual cups with about 1 Tbsp crème fraîche per serving if desired.

Nutrition Snapshot

Per serving: 100 calories, 0g fat, 0g saturated fat, 1g protein, 26g carbs, 2g fiber, 50mg sodium

Vegetarian   Gluten Free

Black Forest Yogurt

If you're thinking you can't have your cake and eat it too, I've got a creamy, low-fat, and much lower-sugar alternative to a Black Forest Cherry Cake. It's inspired by the cake and another German food called *quark*, which is a thick sour cream-like dairy product often combined with fruit as a snack. It is also used to make German-style cheesecake. Greek-style yogurt is about as close as it gets to *quark*, and the cherry-chocolate combination gives us that Black Forest flavor.

4 **Servings**
Total time 5 minutes

3 cups 2-percent Fage yogurt
1 cup Dark Morello Cherries (with juice)
2 oz dark chocolate
Slivered almonds (optional)

1 Spoon ½ cup yogurt into individual serving cups or bowls.

2 Spoon 2 Tbsp cherries and juice onto yogurt. Cover with another ¼ cup yogurt.

3 Grate or simply cut chocolate into small pieces and top each yogurt cup with 1 Tbsp.

4 Serve with a few slivered almonds on top if desired.

Nutrition Snapshot

Per serving: 180 calories, 3g fat, 2g saturated fat,
16g protein, 24g carbs, 1g fiber, 70mg sodium

Recipe Index

Vegetarian Recipe Index

Recipes that are Vegetarian or can easily be made Vegetarian (*)
using simple substitutions

Gluten-free Recipe Index

Recipes that are No-Gluten or can easily be made
No-Gluten (*) using simple substitutions

2-Week Challenge Recipe Index

Recipes that are allowed during the 2-Week Challenge or
are permissible (*) with simple omissions

TJ Store Locations • • • • • • • • • • • • • • • • • •

Arizona

Ahwatukee # 177
4025 E. Chandler Blvd., Ste. 38
Ahwatukee, AZ 85048
Phone: 480-759-2295

Glendale # 085
7720 West Bell Road
Glendale, AZ 85308
Phone: 623-776-7414

Mesa # 089
2050 East Baseline Rd.
Mesa, AZ 85204
Phone: 480-632-0951

Paradise Valley # 282
4726 E. Shea Blvd.
Phoenix, AZ 85028
Phone: 602-485-7788

**Phoenix
(Town & Country) # 090**
4821 N. 20th Street
Phoenix, AZ 85016
Phone: 602-912-9022

Scottsdale (North) # 087
7555 E. Frank Lloyd Wright
N. Scottsdale, AZ 85260
Phone: 480-367-8920

Scottsdale # 094
6202 N. Scottsdale Road
Scottsdale, AZ 85253
Phone: 480-948-9886

Surprise # 092
14095 West Grand Ave.
Surprise, AZ 85374
Phone: 623-546-1640

Tempe # 093
6460 S. McClintock Drive
Tempe, AZ 85283
Phone: 480-838-4142

**Tucson
(Crossroads) # 088**
4766 East Grant Road
Tucson, AZ 85712
Phone: 520-323-4500

**Tucson (Wilmot &
Speedway)# 095**
1101 N. Wilmot Rd.
Suite #147
Tucson, AZ 85712
Phone: 520-733-1313

**Tucson (Campbell &
Limberlost) # 191**
4209 N. Campbell Ave.
Tucson, AZ 85719
Phone: 520-325-0069

Tucson - Oro Valley # 096
7912 N. Oracle
Oro Valley, AZ 85704
Phone: 520-797-4207

California

Agoura Hills
28941 Canwood Street
Agoura Hills, CA 91301
Phone: 818-865-8217

Alameda # 109
2217 South Shore Center
Alameda, CA 94501
Phone: 510-769-5450

Aliso Viejo # 195
The Commons
26541 Aliso Creek Road
Aliso Viejo, CA 92656
Phone: 949-643-5531

Arroyo Grande # 117
955 Rancho Parkway
Arroyo Grande, CA 93420
Phone: 805-474-6114

Bakersfield # 014
8200-C 21 Stockdale Hwy.
Bakersfield, CA 93311
Phone: 661-837-8863

Berkeley #186
1885 University Ave.
Berkeley, CA 94703
Phone: 510-204-9074

Bixby Knolls # 116
4121 Atlantic Ave.
Bixby Knolls, CA 90807
Phone: 562-988-0695

Brea # 011
2500 E. Imperial Hwy.
Suite 177
Brea, CA 92821
Phone 714-257-1180

Brentwood # 201
5451 Lone Tree Way
Brentwood, CA 94513
Phone: 925-516-3044

Burbank # 124
214 East Alameda
Burbank, CA 91502
Phone: 818-848-4299

Camarillo # 114
363 Carmen Drive
Camarillo, CA 93010
Phone: 805-388-1925

Campbell # 073
1875 Bascom Avenue
Campbell, CA 95008
Phone: 408-369-7823

Capitola # 064
3555 Clares Street #D
Capitola, CA 95010
Phone: 831-464-0115

Carlsbad # 220
2629 Gateway Road
Carlsbad, CA 92009
Phone: 760-603-8473

Castro Valley # 084
22224 Redwood Road
Castro Valley, CA 94546
Phone: 510-538-2738

Cathedral City # 118
67-720 East Palm Cyn.
Cathedral City, CA 92234
Phone: 760-202-0090

Cerritos # 104
12861 Towne Center Drive
Cerritos, CA 90703
Phone: 562-402-5148

Chatsworth # 184
10330 Mason Ave.
Chatsworth, CA 91311
Phone: 818-341-3010

Chico # 199
801 East Ave., Suite #110
Chico, CA 95926
Phone: 530-343-9920

Chino Hills # 216
13911 Peyton Dr.
Chino Hills, CA 91709
Phone: 909-627-1404

Chula Vista # 120
878 Eastlake Parkway,
Suite 810
Chula Vista, CA 91914
Phone: 619-656-5370

Claremont # 214
475 W. Foothill Blvd.
Claremont, CA 91711
Phone: 909-625-8784

Clovis # 180
1077 N. Willow, Suite 101
Clovis, CA 93611
Phone: 559-325-3120

**Concord (Oak Grove
& Treat) # 083**
785 Oak Grove Road
Concord, CA 94518
Phone: 925-521-1134

Concord (Airport) # 060
1150 Concord Ave.
Concord, CA 94520
Phone: 925-689-2990

Corona # 213
2790 Cabot Drive, Ste. 165
Corona, CA 92883
Phone: 951-603-0299

Costa Mesa # 035
640 W. 17th Street
Costa Mesa, CA 92627
Phone: 949-642-5134

Culver City # 036
9290 Culver Blvd.
Culver City, CA 90232
Phone: 310-202-1108

Daly City # 074
417 Westlake Center
Daly City, CA 94015
Phone: 650-755-3825

Danville # 065
85 Railroad Ave.
Danville, CA 94526
Phone: 925-838-5757

Davis
885 Russell Blvd.
Davis, CA 95616
Phone: 530-757-2693

Eagle Rock # 055
1566 Colorado Blvd.
Eagle Rock, CA 90041
Phone: 323-257-6422

El Cerrito # 108
225 El Cerrito Plaza
El Cerrito, CA 94530
Phone: 510-524-7609

Cooking with Trader Joe's Cookbook Lighten Up! CookTJ.com

Elk Grove # 190
9670 Bruceville Road
Elk Grove, CA 95757
Phone: 916-686-9980

Emeryville # 072
5700 Christie Avenue
Emeryville, CA 94608
Phone: 510-658-8091

Encinitas # 025
115 N. El Camino Real,
Suite A
Encinitas, CA 92024
Phone: 760-634-2114

Encino # 056
17640 Burbank Blvd.
Encino, CA 91316
Phone: 818-990-7751

Escondido # 105
1885 So. Centre City
Pkwy., Unit "A"
Escondido, CA 92025
Phone: 760-233-4020

Fair Oaks # 071
5309 Sunrise Blvd.
Fair Oaks, CA 95628
Phone: 916-863-1744

Fairfield # 101
1350 Gateway Blvd.,
Suite A1-A7
Fairfield, CA 94533
Phone: 707-434-0144

Folsom # 172
850 East Bidwell
Folsom, CA 95630
Phone: 916-817-8820

Fremont # 077
39324 Argonaut Way
Fremont, CA 94538
Phone: 510-794-1386

Fresno # 008
5376 N. Blackstone
Fresno, CA 93710
Phone: 559-222-4348

Glendale # 053
130 N. Glendale Ave.
Glendale, CA 91206
Phone: 818-637-2990

Goleta # 110
5767 Calle Real
Goleta, CA 93117
Phone: 805-692-2234

Granada Hills # 044
11114 Balboa Blvd.
Granada Hills, CA 91344
Phone: 818-368-6461

Hollywood
1600 N. Vine Street
Los Angeles, CA 90028
Phone: 323-856-0689

Huntington Bch. # 047
18681-101 Main Street
Huntington Bch., CA 92648
Phone: 714-848-9640

Huntington Bch. # 241
21431 Brookhurst St.
Huntington Bch., CA 92646
Phone: 714-968-4070

Huntington Harbor # 244
Huntington Harbour Mall
16821 Algonquin St.
Huntington Bch., CA 92649
Phone: 714-846-7307

Irvine (Walnut Village Center) # 037
14443 Culver Drive
Irvine, CA 92604
Phone: 949-857-8108

Irvine (University Center) # 111
4225 Campus Dr.
Irvine, CA 92612
Phone: 949-509-6138

Irvine (Irvine & Sand Cyn) # 210
6222 Irvine Blvd.
Irvine, CA 92620
Phone: 949-551-6402

La Cañada # 042
475 Foothill Blvd.
La Canada, CA 91011
Phone: 818-790-6373

La Quinta # 189
46-400 Washington Street
La Quinta, CA 92253
Phone: 760-777-1553

Lafayette # 115
3649 Mt. Diablo Blvd.
Lafayette, CA 94549
Phone: 925-299-9344

Laguna Hills # 039
24321 Avenue De La Carlota
Laguna Hills, CA 92653
Phone: 949-586-8453

Laguna Niguel # 103
32351 Street of the Golden
Lantern
Laguna Niguel, CA 92677
Phone: 949-493-8599

La Jolla # 020
8657 Villa LaJolla
Drive #210
La Jolla, CA 92037
Phone: 858-546-8629

La Mesa # 024
5495 Grossmont Center Dr.
La Mesa, CA 91942
Phone: 619-466-0105

Larkspur # 235
2052 Redwood Hwy
Larkspur, CA 94921
Phone: 415-945-7955

Livermore # 208
1122-A East Stanley Blvd.
Livermore, CA 94550
Phone: 925-243-1947

Long Beach (PCH) # 043
6451 E. Pacific Coast Hwy.
Long Beach, CA 90803
Phone: 562-596-4388

Long Beach (Bellflower Blvd.) # 194
2222 Bellflower Blvd.
Long Beach, CA 90815
Phone: 562-596-2514

Los Altos # 127
2310 Homestead Rd.
Los Altos, CA 94024
Phone: 408-245-1917

Los Angeles (Silver Lake) # 017
2738 Hyperion Ave.
Los Angeles, CA 90027
Phone: 323-665-6774

Los Angeles # 031
263 S. La Brea
Los Angeles, CA 90036
Phone: 323-965-1989

Los Angeles (Sunset Strip) # 192
8000 Sunset Blvd.
Los Angeles, CA 90046
Phone: 323-822-7663

Los Gatos # 181
15466 Los Gatos Blvd.
Los Gatos, CA 95032
Phone 408-356-2324

Manhattan Beach # 034
1821 Manhattan
Beach. Blvd.
Manhattan Bch., CA 90266
Phone: 310-372-1274

Manhattan Beach # 196
1800 Rosecrans Blvd.
Manhattan Beach,
CA 90266
Phone: 310-725-9800

Menlo Park # 069
720 Menlo Avenue
Menlo Park, CA 94025
Phone: 650-323-2134

Millbrae # 170
765 Broadway
Millbrae, CA 94030
Phone: 650-259-9142

Mission Viejo # 126
25410 Marguerite Parkway
Mission Viejo, CA 92692
Phone: 949-581-5638

Modesto # 009
3250 Dale Road
Modesto, CA 95356
Phone: 209-491-0445

Monrovia # 112
604 W. Huntington Dr.
Monrovia, CA 91016
Phone: 626-358-8884

Monterey # 204
570 Munras Ave., Ste. 20
Monterey, CA 93940
Phone: 831-372-2010

Montrose
2462 Honolulu Ave.
Montrose, CA 91020
Phone: 818-957-3613

Morgan Hill # 202
17035 Laurel Road
Morgan Hill, CA 95037
Phone: 408-778-6409

Mountain View # 081
590 Showers Dr.
Mountain View, CA 94040
Phone: 650-917-1013

Napa # 128
3654 Bel Aire Plaza
Napa, CA 94558
Phone: 707-256-0806

Newbury Park # 243
125 N. Reino Road
Newbury Park, CA
Phone: 805-375-1984

Newport Beach # 125
8086 East Coast Highway
Newport Beach, CA 92657
Phone: 949-494-7404

Novato # 198
7514 Redwood Blvd.
Novato, CA 94945
Phone: 415-898-9359

**Oakland
(Lakeshore) # 203**
3250 Lakeshore Ave.
Oakland, CA 94610
Phone: 510-238-9076

**Oakland
(Rockridge) # 231**
5727 College Ave.
Oakland, CA 94618
Phone: 510-923-9428

Oceanside # 22
2570 Vista Way
Oceanside, CA 92054
Phone: 760-433-9994

Orange # 046
2114 N. Tustin St.
Orange, CA 92865
Phone: 714-283-5697

Pacific Grove # 008
1170 Forest Avenue
Pacific Grove, CA 93950
Phone: 831-656-0180

Palm Desert # 003
44-250 Town Center Way,
Suite C6
Palm Desert, CA 92260
Phone: 760-340-2291

Palmdale # 185
39507 10th Street West
Palmdale, CA 93551
Phone: 661-947-2890

Palo Alto # 207
855 El Camino Real
Palo Alto, CA 94301
Phone: 650-327-7018

**Pasadena
(S. Lake Ave.) # 179**
345 South Lake Ave.
Pasadena, CA 91101
Phone: 626-395-9553

**Pasadena
(S. Arroyo Pkwy.) # 051**
610 S. Arroyo Parkway
Pasadena, CA 91105
Phone: 626-568-9254

**Pasadena
(Hastings Ranch) # 171**
467 Rosemead Blvd.
Pasadena, CA 91107
Phone: 626-351-3399

Petaluma # 107
169 North McDowell Blvd.
Petaluma, CA 94954
Phone: 707-769-2782

Pinole # 230
2742 Pinole Valley Rd.
Pinole, CA 94564
Phone: 510-222-3501

Pleasanton # 066
4040 Pimlico #150
Pleasanton, CA 94588
Phone: 925-225-3600

Rancho Cucamonga # 217
6401 Haven Ave.
Rancho Cucamonga,
CA 91737
Phone: 909-476-1410

**Rancho Palos Verdes
057**
28901 S. Western Ave. #243
Rancho Palos Verdes,
CA 90275
Phone: 310-832-1241

Rancho Palos Verdes # 233
31176 Hawthorne Blvd.
Rancho Palos Verdes,
CA 90275
Phone: 310-544-1727

**Rancho Santa
Margarita # 027**
30652 Santa Margarita Pkwy.
Suite F102
Rancho Santa Margarita,
CA 92688
Phone: 949-888-3640

Redding # 219
845 Browning St.
Redding, CA 96003
Phone: 530-223-4875

Redlands # 099
552 Orange Street Plaza
Redlands, CA 92374
Phone: 909-798-3888

Redondo Beach # 038
1761 S. Elena Avenue
Redondo Bch., CA 90277
Phone: 310-316-1745

Riverside # 15
6225 Riverside Plaza
Riverside, CA 92506
Phone: 951-682-4684

Roseville # 80
1117 Roseville Square
Roseville, CA 95678
Phone: 916-784-9084

**Sacramento
(Folsom Blvd.) # 175**
5000 Folsom Blvd.
Sacramento, CA 95819
Phone: 916-456-1853

**Sacramento
(Fulton & Marconi) # 070**
2625 Marconi Avenue
Sacramento, CA 95821
Phone: 916-481-8797

San Carlos # 174
1482 El Camino Real
San Carlos, CA 94070
Phone: 650-594-2138

San Clemente # 016
638 Camino DeLosMares,
Sp.#115-G
San Clemente, CA 92673
Phone: 949-240-9996

**San Diego
(Hillcrest) # 026**
1090 University Ste.
G100-107
San Diego, CA 92103
Phone: 619-296-3122

**San Diego
(Point Loma) # 188**
2401 Truxtun Rd., Ste. 300
San Diego, CA 92106
Phone: 619-758-9272

**San Diego
(Pacific Beach) # 021**
1211 Garnet Avenue
San Diego, CA 92109
Phone: 858-272-7235

**San Diego (Carmel
Mtn. Ranch) # 023**
11955 Carmel Mtn. Rd. #702
San Diego, CA 92128
Phone: 858-673-0526

**San Diego
(Scripps Ranch) # 221**
9850 Hibert Street
San Diego, CA 92131
Phone: 858-549-9185

San Dimas # 028
856 Arrow Hwy. "C"
Target Center
San Dimas, CA 91773
Phone: 909-305-4757

**San Francisco
(9th Street) # 078**
555 9th Street
San Francisco, CA 94103
Phone: 415-863-1292

**San Francisco
(Masonic Ave.) # 100**
3 Masonic Avenue
San Francisco, CA 94118
Phone: 415-346-9964

**San Francisco
(North Beach) # 019**
401 Bay Street
San Francisco, CA 94133
Phone: 415-351-1013

**San Francisco
(Stonestown) # 236**
265 Winston Dr.
San Francisco, CA 94132
Phone: 415-665-1835

San Gabriel # 032
7260 N. Rosemead Blvd.
San Gabriel, CA 91775
Phone: 626-285-5862

San Jose (Bollinger) # 232
7250 Bollinger Rd.
San Jose, CA 95129
Phone: 408-873-7384

**San Jose
(Coleman Ave) # 212**
635 Coleman Ave.
San Jose, CA 95110
Phone: 408-298-9731

**San Jose
(Old Almaden) # 063**
5353 Almaden Expressway
#J-38
San Jose, CA 95118
Phone: 408-927-9091

**San Jose
(Westgate West) # 062**
5269 Prospect
San Jose, CA 95129
Phone: 408-446-5055

San Luis Obispo # 041
3977 Higuera Street
San Luis Obispo, CA 93401
Phone: 805-783-2780

**San Mateo
(Grant Street) # 067**
1820-22 S. Grant Street
San Mateo, CA 94402
Phone: 650-570-6140

**San Mateo
(Hillsdale) # 245**
45 W Hillsdale Blvd
San Mateo, CA 94403
Phone: 650-286-1509

San Rafael # 061
337 Third Street
San Rafael, CA 94901
Phone: 415-454-9530

Santa Ana # 113
3329 South Bristol Street
Santa Ana, CA 92704
Phone: 714-424-9304

**Santa Barbara
(S. Milpas St.) # 059**
29 S. Milpas Street
Santa Barbara, CA 93103
Phone: 805-564-7878

**Santa Barbara
(De La Vina) # 183**
3025 De La Vina
Santa Barbara, CA 93105
Phone: 805-563-7383

Santa Cruz # 193
700 Front Street
Santa Cruz, CA 95060
Phone: 831-425-0140

Santa Maria # 239
1303 S. Bradley Road
Santa Maria, CA 93454
Phone: 805-925-1657

Santa Monica # 006
3212 Pico Blvd.
Santa Monica, CA 90405
Phone: 310-581-0253

**Santa Rosa
(Cleveland Ave.) # 075**
3225 Cleveland Avenue
Santa Rosa, CA 95403
Phone: 707-525-1406

**Santa Rosa
(Santa Rosa Ave.) # 178**
2100 Santa Rosa Ave.
Santa Rosa, CA 95407
Phone: 707-535-0788

Sherman Oaks # 049
14119 Riverside Drive
Sherman Oaks, CA 91423
Phone: 818-789-2771

Simi Valley # 030
2975-A Cochran St.
Simi Valley, CA 93065
Phone: 805-520-3135

South Pasadena # 018
613 Mission Street
South Pasadena, CA 91030
Phone: 626-441-6263

**South San Francisco
187**
301 McLellan Dr.
So. San Francisco,
CA 94080
Phone: 650-583-6401

Stockton # 076
6535 Pacific Avenue
Stockton, CA 95207
Phone: 209-951-7597

Studio City # 122
11976 Ventura Blvd.
Studio City, CA 91604
Phone: 818-509-0168

Sunnyvale # 068
727 Sunnyvale/
Saratoga Rd.
Sunnyvale, CA 94087
Phone: 408-481-9082

Temecula # 102
40665 Winchester Rd., Bldg.
B, Ste. 4-6
Temecula, CA 92591
Phone: 951-296-9964

Templeton # 211
1111 Rossi Road
Templeton, CA 93465
Phone: 805-434-9562

Thousand Oaks # 196
451 Avenida
De Los Arboles
Thousand Oaks, CA 91360
Phone: 805-492-7107

Toluca Lake # 054
10130 Riverside Drive
Toluca Lake, CA 91602
Phone: 818-762-2787

**Torrance
(Hawthorne Blvd.) # 121**
19720 Hawthorne Blvd.
Torrance, CA 90503
Phone: 310-793-8585

**Torrance (Rolling
Hills Plaza) # 029**
2545 Pacific Coast Highway
Torrance, CA 90505
Phone: 310-326-9520

Tustin # 197
12932 Newport Avenue
Tustin, CA 92780
Phone: 714-669-3752

Upland # 010
333 So. Mountain Avenue
Upland, CA 91786
Phone: 909-946-4799

Valencia # 013
26517 Bouquet Canyon Rd
Santa Clarita, CA 91350
Phone: 661-263-3796

Ventura # 045
1795 S. Victoria Avenue
Ventura, CA 93003
Phone: 805-650-9977

Ventura – Midtown
103 S. Mills Road Suite 104
Ventura, CA 93003
Phone: 805-658-2664

Walnut Creek # 123
1372 So. California Blvd.
Walnut Creek, CA 94596
Phone: 925-945-1674

West Hills # 050
6751 Fallbrook Ave.
West Hills, CA 91307
Phone: 818-347-2591

West Hollywood # 040
7304 Santa Monica Blvd.
West Hollywood, CA 90046
Phone: 323-851-9772

West Hollywood # 173
8611 Santa Monica Blvd.
West Hollywood, CA 90069
Phone: 310-657-0152

**West Los Angeles
(National Blvd.) # 007**
10850 National Blvd.
West Los Angeles, CA 90064
Phone: 310-470-1917

**West Los Angeles
S. Sepulveda Blvd.) # 119**
3456 S. Sepulveda Blvd.
West Los Angeles,
CA 90034
Phone: 310-836-2458

**West Los Angeles
(Olympic) # 215**
11755 W. Olympic Blvd.
West Los Angeles,
CA 90064
Phone: 310-477-5949

Westchester # 033
8645 S. Sepulveda
Westchester, CA 90045
Phone: 310-338-9238

Westlake Village # 058
3835 E. Thousand
Oaks Blvd.
Westlake Village, CA 91362
Phone: 805-494-5040

Westwood # 234
1000 Glendon Avenue
Los Angeles, CA 90024
Phone: 310-824-1495

Whittier # 048
15025 E. Whittier Blvd.
Whittier, CA 90603
Phone: 562-698-1642

Woodland Hills # 209
21054 Clarendon St.
Woodland Hills, CA 91364
Phone: 818-712-9475

Yorba Linda # 176
19655 Yorba Linda Blvd.
Yorba Linda, CA 92886
Phone: 714-970-0116

Connecticut

Danbury # 525
113 Mill Plain Rd.
Danbury, CT 06811
Phone: 203-739-0098
Alcohol: Beer Only

Darien # 522
436 Boston Post Rd.
Darien, CT 06820
Phone: 203-656-1414
Alcohol: Beer Only

Fairfield # 523
2258 Black Rock Turnpike
Fairfield, CT 06825
Phone: 203-330-8301
Alcohol: Beer Only

Orange # 524
560 Boston Post Road
Orange, CT 06477
Phone: 203-795-5505
Alcohol: Beer Only

West Hartford # 526
1489 New Britain Ave.
West Hartford, CT 06110
Phone: 860-561-4771
Alcohol: Beer Only

Westport # 521
400 Post Road East
Westport, CT 06880
Phone: 203-226-8966
Alcohol: Beer Only

Delaware

Wilmington* # 536
5605 Concord Pike
Wilmington, DE 19803
Phone: 302-478-8494

District of Columbia

Washington # 653
1101 25th Street NW
Washington, DC 20037
Phone: 202-296-1921

Florida

Naples – coming soon!
10600 Tamiami Trail North
Naples, FL 34108
Phone: TBD

Georgia

Athens
1850 Epps Bridge Parkway
Athens, GA 30606
Phone: 706-583-8934

**Atlanta
(Buckhead) # 735**
3183 Peachtree Rd NE
Atlanta, GA 30305
Phone: 404-842-0907

Atlanta (Midtown) # 730
931 Monroe Dr., NE
Atlanta, GA 30308
Phone: 404-815-9210

Marietta # 732
4250 Roswell Road
Marietta, GA 30062
Phone: 678-560-3585

Norcross # 734
5185 Peachtree Parkway, Bld.
1200
Norcross, GA 30092
Phone: 678-966-9236

Roswell # 733
635 W. Crossville Road
Roswell, GA 30075
Phone: 770-645-8505

Sandy Springs # 731
6277 Roswell Road NE
Sandy Springs, GA 30328
Phone: 404-236-2414

Illinois

Algonquin # 699
1800 South Randall Road
Algonquin, IL 60102
Phone: 847-854-4886

Arlington Heights # 687
17 W. Rand Road
Arlington Heights, IL 60004
Phone: 847-506-0752

Batavia # 689
1942 West Fabyan
Parkway #222
Batavia, IL 60510
Phone: 630-879-3234

Chicago (Diversey Pkwy)
667 W. Diversey Pkwy
Chicago, IL 60614
Phone: 773-935-7255

**Chicago
(Lincoln & Grace) # 688**
3745 North Lincoln Avenue
Chicago, IL 60613
Phone: 773-248-4920

**Chicago
(Lincoln Park) # 691**
1840 North Clybourn
Avenue #200
Chicago, IL 60614
Phone: 312-274-9733

**Chicago
(River North) # 696**
44 E. Ontario St.
Chicago, IL 60611
Phone: 312-951-6369

Chicago (South Loop)
1147 S. Wabash Ave.
Chicago, IL 60605
Phone: 312-588-0489

Downers Grove # 683
122 Ogden Ave.
Downers Grove, IL 60515
Phone: 630-241-1662

Glen Ellyn # 680
680 Roosevelt Rd.
Glen Ellyn, IL 60137
Phone: 630-858-5077

Glenview # 681
1407 Waukegan Road

Glenview, IL 60025
Phone: 847-657-7821

La Grange # 685
25 North La Grange Road
La Grange, IL 60525
Phone: 708-579-0838

Lake Zurich # 684
735 W. Route 22**
Lake Zurich, IL 60047
Phone: 847-550-7827
[**For accurate driving
directions using
GPS, please use
735 W Main Street]

Naperville # 690
44 West Gartner Road
Naperville, IL 60540
Phone: 630-355-4389

Northbrook # 682
127 Skokie Blvd.
Northbrook, IL 60062
Phone: 847-498-9076

Oak Park # 697
483 N. Harlem Ave.
Oak Park, IL 60301
Phone: 708-386-1169

Orland Park # 686
14924 S. La Grange Road
Orland Park, IL 60462
Phone: 708-349-9021

Park Ridge # 698
190 North Northwest Hwy
Park Ridge, IL 60068
Phone: 847-292-1108

Indiana

**Indianapolis
(Castleton) # 671**
5473 East 82nd Street
Indianapolis, IN 46250
Phone: 317-595-8950

**Indianapolis
(West 86th) # 670**
2902 West 86th Street
Indianapolis, IN 46268
Phone: 317-337-1880

Iowa

West Des Moines
6305 Mills Civic Parkway
West Des Moines, IA 50266
Phone: 515-225-3820

Kentucky

Louisville
4600 Shelbyville Road
Louisville, KY 40207
Phone: 502-895-1361

Kansas

Leawood* #723
4201 W 119th Street
Leawood, KS 66209
Phone: 913-327-7209

Maine

Portland # 519
87 Marginal Way
Portland, ME 04101
Phone: 207-699-3799

Maryland

Annapolis* # 650
160 F Jennifer Road
Annapolis, MD 21401
Phone: 410-573-0505

Bethesda* # 645
6831 Wisconsin Avenue
Bethesda, MD 20815
Phone: 301-907-0982

Columbia* # 658
6610 Marie Curie Dr.
(Int. of 175 & 108)
Elkridge, MD 21075
Phone: 410-953-8139

Gaithersburg* # 648
18270 Contour Rd.
Gaithersburg, MD 20877
Phone: 301-947-5953

Pikesville* # 655
1809 Reisterstown Road, Suite
#121
Pikesville, MD 21208
Phone: 410-484-8373

Rockville* # 642
12268-H Rockville Pike
Rockville, MD 20852
Phone: 301-468-6656

Silver Spring* # 652
10741 Columbia Pike
Silver Spring, MD 20901
Phone: 301-681-1675

Towson* # 649
1 E. Joppa Rd.
Towson, MD 21286
Phone: 410-296-9851

Massachusetts

Acton* # 511
145 Great Road
Acton, MA 01720
Phone: 978-266-8908

Arlington* # 505
1427 Massachusetts Ave.
Arlington, MA 02476
Phone: 781-646-9138

Boston #510
899 Boylston Street
Boston, MA 02115
Phone: 617-262-6505

Brookline # 501
1317 Beacon Street
Brookline, MA 02446
Phone: 617-278-9997

Burlington* # 515
51 Middlesex Turnpike
Burlington, MA 01803
Phone: 781-273-2310

Cambridge
748 Memorial Drive
Cambridge, MA 02139
Phone: 617-491-8582

**Cambridge
(Fresh Pond)* # 517**
211 Alewife Brook Pkwy
Cambridge, MA 02138
Phone: 617-498-3201

Framingham # 503
659 Worcester Road
Framingham, MA 01701
Phone: 508-935-2931

Hadley* # 512
375 Russell Street
Hadley, MA 01035
Phone: 413-587-3260

Hanover* # 513
1775 Washington Street
Hanover, MA 02339
Phone: 781-826-5389

Hyannis* # 514
Christmas Tree Promenade
655 Route 132, Unit 4-A
Hyannis, MA 02601
Phone: 508-790-3008

Needham Hts* 504
958 Highland Avenue
Needham Hts, MA 02494
Phone: 781-449-6993

Peabody* # 516
300 Andover Street,
Suite 15
Peabody, MA 01960
Phone: 978-977-5316

Saugus* # 506
358 Broadway, Unit B
(Shops @ Saugus, Rte. 1)
Saugus, MA 01906
Phone: 781-231-0369

Shrewsbury* # 508
77 Boston Turnpike
Shrewsbury, MA 01545
Phone: 508-755-9560

Tyngsboro* # 507
440 Middlesex Road
Tyngsboro, MA 01879
Phone: 978-649-2726

West Newton* # 509
1121 Washington St.
West Newton, MA 02465
Phone: 617-244-1620

Michigan

Ann Arbor # 678
2398 East Stadium Blvd.
Ann Arbor, MI 48104
Phone: 734-975-2455

Farmington Hills # 675
31221 West 14 Mile Road
Farmington Hills, MI 48334
Phone: 248-737-4609

Grosse Pointe # 665
17028 Kercheval Ave.
Grosse Pointe, MI 48230
Phone: 313-640-7794

Northville # 667
20490 Haggerty Road
Northville, MI 48167
Phone: 734-464-3675

Rochester Hills # 668
3044 Walton Blvd.
Rochester Hills, MI 48309
Phone: 248-375-2190

Royal Oak # 674
27880 Woodward Ave.
Royal Oak, MI 48067
Phone: 248-582-9002

Minnesota

Maple Grove # 713
12105 Elm Creek Blvd. N.
Maple Grove, MN 55369
Phone: 763-315-1739

Minnetonka # 714
11220 Wayzata Blvd
Minnetonka, MN 55305
Phone: 952-417-9080

Rochester
1200 16th St. SW
Rochester, NY 55902
Phone: 952-417-9080

St. Louis Park # 710
4500 Excelsior Blvd.
St. Louis Park, MN 55416
Phone: 952-285-1053

St. Paul # 716
484 Lexington Parkway S.
St. Paul, MN 55116
Phone: 651-698-3119

Woodbury # 715
8960 Hudson Road
Woodbury, MN 55125
Phone: 651-735-0269

Missouri

Brentwood # 792
48 Brentwood
Promenade Court
Brentwood, MO 63144
Phone: 314-963-0253

Chesterfield # 693
1679 Clarkson Road
Chesterfield, MO 63017
Phone: 636-536-7846

Creve Coeur # 694
11505 Olive Blvd.
Creve Coeur, MO 63141
Phone: 314-569-0427

*Store does not carry alcohol.

Des Peres # 695
13343 Manchester Rd.
Des Peres, MO 63131
Phone: 314-984-5051

Kansas City
8600 Ward Parkway
Kansas City, MO 64114
Phone: 816-333-5322

Nebraska

Lincoln
3120 Pine Lake Road,
Suite R
Lincoln, NE 68516
Phone: 402-328-0120

Omaha # 714
10305 Pacific St.
Omaha, NE 68114
Phone: 402-391-3698

Nevada

Anthem # 280
10345 South Eastern Ave.
Henderson, NV 89052
Phone: 702-407-8673

Carson City # 281
3790 US Highway 395 S,
Suite 401
Carson City, NV 89705
Phone: 775-267-2486

Henderson # 097
2716 North Green Valley
Parkway
Henderson, NV 89014
Phone: 702-433-6773

**Las Vegas
(Decatur Blvd.) # 098**
2101 S. Decatur Blvd.,
Suite 25
Las Vegas, NV 89102
Phone: 702-367-0227

**Las Vegas
(Summerlin) # 086**
7575 West Washington, Suite
117
Las Vegas, NV 89128
Phone: 702-242-8240

Reno # 082
5035 S. McCarran Blvd.
Reno, NV 89502
Phone: 775-826-1621

New Jersey

Edgewater* # 606
715 River Road
Edgewater, NJ 07020
Phone: 201-945-5932

Florham Park* # 604
186 Columbia Turnpike
Florham Park, NJ 07932
Phone: 973-514-1511

Marlton* # 631
300 P Route 73 South
Marlton, NJ 08053
Phone: 856-988-3323

Millburn* # 609
187 Millburn Ave.
Millburn, NJ 07041
Phone: 973-218-0912

Paramus* # 605
404 Rt. 17 North
Paramus, NJ 07652
Phone: 201-265-9624

Princeton # 607
3528 US 1
(Brunswick Pike)
Princeton, NJ 08540
Phone: 609-897-0581

Shrewsbury*
1031 Broad St.
Shrewsbury, NJ 07702
Phone: 732-389-2535

Wayne* # 632
1172 Hamburg Turnpike
Wayne, NJ 07470
Phone: 973-692-0050

Westfield # 601
155 Elm St.
Westfield, NJ 07090
Phone: 908-301-0910

Westwood* # 602
20 Irvington Street
Westwood, NJ 07675
Phone: 201-263-0134

New Mexico

Albuquerque # 166
8928 Holly Ave. NE
Albuquerque, NM 87122
Phone: 505-796-0311

**Albuquerque
(Uptown) # 167**
2200 Uptown Loop NE
Albuquerque, NM 87110
Phone: 505-883-3662

Santa Fe # 165
530 W. Cordova Road
Santa Fe, NM 87505
Phone: 505-995-8145

New York

Brooklyn # 558
130 Court St
Brooklyn, NY 11201
Phone: 718-246-8460
Alcohol: Beer Only

Commack # 551
5010 Jericho Turnpike
Commack, NY 11725
Phone: 631-493-9210
Alcohol: Beer Only

Hartsdale # 533
215 North Central Avenue
Hartsdale, NY 10530
Phone: 914-997-1960
Alcohol: Beer Only

Hewlett # 554
1280 West Broadway
Hewlett, NY 11557
Phone: 516-569-7191
Alcohol: Beer Only

Lake Grove # 556
137 Alexander Ave.
Lake Grove, NY 11755
Phone: 631-863-2477
Alcohol: Beer Only

Larchmont # 532
1260 Boston Post Road
Larchmont, NY 10538
Phone: 914-833-9110
Alcohol: Beer Only

Merrick # 553
1714 Merrick Road
Merrick, NY 11566
Phone: 516-771-1012
Alcohol: Beer Only

**New York
(72nd & Broadway) # 542**
2075 Broadway
New York, NY 10023
Phone: 212-799-0028
Alcohol: Beer Only

**New York
(Chelsea) # 543**
675 6th Ave
New York, NY 10010
Phone: 212-255-2106
Alcohol: Beer Only

**New York (Union Square
Grocery) # 540**
142 E. 14th St.
New York, NY 10003
Phone: 212-529-4612
Alcohol: Beer Only

**New York (Union Square
Wine) # 541**
138 E. 14th St.
New York, NY 10003
Phone: 212-529-6326
Alcohol: Wine Only

Oceanside # 552
3418 Long Beach Rd.
Oceanside, NY 11572
Phone: 516-536-9163
Alcohol: Beer Only

Plainview # 555
425 S. Oyster Bay Rd.
Plainview, NY 11803
Phone: 516-933-6900
Alcohol: Beer Only

Queens # 557
90-30 Metropolitan Ave.
Queens, NY 11374
Phone: 718-275-1791
Alcohol: Beer Only

Scarsdale # 531
727 White Plains Rd.
Scarsdale, NY 10583
Phone: 914-472-2988
Alcohol: Beer Only

Staten Island
2385 Richmond Ave
Staten Island, NY 10314
Phone: 718-370-1085
Alcohol: Beer Only

North Carolina

Cary # 741
1393 Kildaire Farms Rd.
Cary, NC 27511
Phone: 919-465-5984

Chapel Hill # 745
1800 E. Franklin St.
Chapel Hill, NC 27514
Phone: 919-918-7871

**Charlotte
(Midtown) # 744**
1133 Metropolitan Ave., Ste.
100
Charlotte, NC 28204
Phone: 704-334-0737

Charlotte (North) # 743
1820 East Arbors Dr.**
(corner of W. Mallard Creek
Church Rd. & Senator
Royall Dr.)
Charlotte, NC 28262
Phone: 704-688-9578
[**For accurate driving
directions on the web, please
use 1820 W. Mallard Creek
Church Rd.]

Charlotte (South) # 742
6418 Rea Rd.
Charlotte, NC 28277
Phone: 704-543-5249

Raleigh # 746
3000 Wake Forest Rd.
Raleigh, NC 27609
Phone: 919-981-7422

Ohio

Cincinnati # 669
7788 Montgomery Road
Cincinnati, OH 45236
Phone: 513-984-3452

Columbus # 679
3888 Townsfair Way
Columbus, OH 43219
Phone: 614-473-0794

Dublin # 672
6355 Sawmill Road
Dublin, OH 43017
Phone: 614-793-8505

Kettering # 673
328 East Stroop Road
Kettering, OH 45429
Phone: 937-294-5411

Westlake # 677
175 Market Street
Westlake, OH 44145
Phone: 440-250-1592

Woodmere # 676
28809 Chagrin Blvd.
Woodmere, OH 44122
Phone: 216-360-9320

Oregon

Beaverton # 141
11753 S. W. Beaverton Hillsdale Hwy.
Beaverton, OR 97005
Phone: 503-626-3794

Bend # 150
63455 North
Highway 97, Ste. 4
Bend, OR 97701
Phone: 541-312-4198

Clackamas # 152
9345 SE 82nd Ave (across
from Home Depot)
Happy Valley, OR 97086
Phone: 503-771-6300

Corvallis # 154
1550 NW 9th Street
Corvallis, OR 97330
Phone: 541-753-0048

Eugene # 145
85 Oakway Center
Eugene, OR 97401
Phone: 541-485-1744

Hillsboro # 149
2285 NW 185th Ave.
Hillsboro, OR 97124
Phone: 503-645-8321

Lake Oswego # 142
15391 S. W. Bangy Rd.
Lake Oswego, OR 97035
Phone: 503-639-3238

Portland (SE) # 143
4715 S. E. 39th Avenue
Portland, OR 97202
Phone: 503-777-1601

Portland (NW) # 146
2122 N.W. Glisan
Portland, OR 97210
Phone: 971-544-0788

**Portland
(Hollywood) # 144**
4121 N.E. Halsey St.
Portland, OR 97213
Phone: 503-284-1694

Salem #153
4450 Commercial St.,
Suite 100
Salem, OR 97302
Phone: 503-378-9042

Pennsylvania

Ardmore* # 635
112 Coulter Avenue
Ardmore, PA 19003
Phone: 610-658-0645

Jenkintown* # 633
933 Old York Road
Jenkintown, PA 19046
Phone: 215-885-524

Media* # 637
12 East State Street
Media, PA 19063
Phone: 610-891-2752

North Wales* # 639
1430 Bethlehem Pike
(corner SR 309 & SR 63)
North Wales, PA 19454
Phone: 215-646-5870

Philadelphia* # 634
2121 Market Street
Philadelphia, PA 19103
Phone: 215-569-9282

Pittsburgh* # 638
6343 Penn Ave.
Pittsburgh, PA 15206
Phone: 412-363-5748

Pittsburgh*
1630 Washington Road
Pittsburgh, PA 15228
Phone: 412-835-2212

State College* - coming soon!
1855 North Atherton St.
State College, PA 16803
Phone: TBD

Wayne* # 632
171 East Swedesford Rd.
Wayne, PA 19087
Phone: 610-225-0925

Rhode Island

Warwick* # 518
1000 Bald Hill Rd
Warwick, RI 02886
Phone: 401-821-5368

South Carolina

Greenville
59 Woodruff
Industrial Lane
Greenville, SC 29607
Phone: 864-286-0231

Mt. Pleasant – #752
401 Johnnie Dodds Blvd.
Mt. Pleasant, SC 29464
Phone: 843-884-4037

Tennessee

Nashville # 664
3909 Hillsboro Pike
Nashville, TN 37215
Phone: 615-297-6560
Alcohol: Beer Only

Virginia

Alexandria # 647
612 N. Saint Asaph Street
Alexandria, VA 22314
Phone: 703-548-0611

Bailey's Crossroads # 644
5847 Leesburg Pike
Bailey's Crossroads,
VA 22041
Phone: 703-379-5883

Centreville # 654
14100 Lee Highway
Centreville, VA 20120
Phone: 703-815-0697

Clarendon
1109 N. Highland St.
Arlington, VA 22201
Phone: 703-351-8015

Fairfax # 643
9464 Main Street
Fairfax, VA 22031
Phone: 703-764-8550

Falls Church # 641
7514 Leesburg Turnpike
Falls Church, VA 22043
Phone: 703-288-0566

Newport News # 656
12551 Jefferson Ave.,
Suite #179
Newport News, VA 23602
Phone: 757-890-0235

*Store does not carry alcohol.

Reston # 646
11958 Killingsworth Ave.
Reston, VA 20194
Phone: 703-689-0865

**Richmond
(Short Pump) # 659**
11331 W Broad St, Ste 161
Glen Allen, VA 23060
Phone: 804-360-4098

Springfield # 651
6394 Springfield Plaza
Springfield, VA 22150
Phone: 703-569-9301

Virginia Beach # 660
503 Hilltop Plaza
Virginia Beach, VA 23454
Phone: 757-422-4840

Williamsburg # 657
5000 Settlers Market Blvd
(corner of Monticello and
Settlers Market)**
Williamsburg, VA 23188
Phone: 757-259-2135
[**For accurate driving
directions on the web, please
use 5224 Monticello Ave.]

Washington

Ballard # 147
4609 14th Avenue NW
Seattle, WA 98107
Phone: 206-783-0498

Bellevue # 131
15400 N. E. 20th Street
Bellevue, WA 98007
Phone: 425-643-6885

Bellingham # 151
2410 James Street
Bellingham, WA 98225
Phone: 360-734-5166

Burien # 133
15868 1st. Avenue South
Burien, WA 98148
Phone: 206-901-9339

Everett # 139
811 S.E. Everett Mall Way
Everett, WA 98208
Phone: 425-513-2210

Federal Way # 134
1758 S. 320th Street
Federal Way, WA 98003
Phone: 253-529-9242

Issaquah # 138
1495 11th Ave. N.W.
Issaquah, WA 98027
Phone: 425-837-8088

Kirkland # 132
12632 120th Avenue N. E.
Kirkland, WA 98034
Phone: 425-823-1685

Lynnwood # 129
19500 Highway 99,
Suite 100
Lynnwood, WA 98036
Phone: 425-744-1346

Olympia # 156
Olympia West Center
1530 Black Lake Blvd.
Olympia, WA 98502
Phone: 360-352-7440

Redmond # 140
15932 Redmond Way
Redmond, WA 98052
Phone: 425-883-1624

Seattle (U. District) # 137
4555 Roosevelt Way NE
Seattle, WA 98105
Phone: 206-547-6299

**Seattle
(Queen Anne Hill) # 135**
112 West Galer St.
Seattle, WA 98119
Phone: 206-378-5536

Seattle (Capitol Hill) # 130
1700 Madison St.
Seattle, WA 98122
Phone: 206-322-7268

Silverdale
9991 Mickelberry Rd.
Silverdale, WA 98383
Phone: 360-307-7224

Spokane
2975 East 29th Avenue
Spokane, WA 99223
Phone: 509-534-1077

University Place # 148
3800 Bridgeport Way West
University Place, WA 98466
Phone: 253-460-2672

Vancouver # 136
305 SE Chkalov Drive #B1
Vancouver, WA 98683
Phone: 360-883-9000

Wisconsin

Glendale # 711
5600 North Port
Washington Road
Glendale, WI 53217
Phone: 414-962-3382

Madison # 712
1810 Monroe Street
Madison, WI 53711
Phone: 608-257-1916

*Although we aim to ensure that the store location
information contained here is correct, we will not be
responsible for any errors or omissions.*

Photo Credits

All photos of recipes © by Dan Komoda

By **shutterstock.com** on pages: 18 © Irmak Akcadogan/ 85 © Albo003/ 44 © Hintau Aliaksei/ 38 © Amalia19/ 81 © Aaron Amat/ cover, 6, 8, 27, 41, 45, 73, 165, 207, 212, 225, 248 © Andrjuss/ 52, 248 © Allgusak/ 19 © Artjazz/ 185 © Teresa Azevedo/ 111, 153, 231, 233, 236 © Baldyrgan/ 44, 190, 195, 206, 218 © Lucy Baldwin/ 42 © Beata Becla/ 65 © Nikola Bilic/ 206, 207 © Bomshtein/ 176, 219 © Bonchan/ 26, 33, 118, 138, 147 © Bonsai/ 179 © Buriy/ 21 © Diego Cervo/ 130 © Chiyacat/ 2, 12, 15, 16, 21, 27, 36, 38, 44, 81, 156, 162, 170, 172, 192, 200, 206, 216, 222, 225, 247 © Cyrrpit/ 50, 190 © Dionisvera/ 74 © Barbara Dudzinska/ 13, 21, 92, 222 © Elena Elisseeva/ 164, 167, 168, 173, 186 © Ensuper/ 170 © Rustam R. Fazlaev/ 95 © Eric Gevaert/ 16, © Angelo Gilardelli/ 226 © Jaroslaw Grudzinski/ 246 © Robert Gubbins/ 21 © 2happy/ 28, 210 © Haveseen/ 2, 14, 15, 23, © javarman/ 153, 216 © Jiri Hera/ 73 © Jiang Hongyan/ 164 © iBoat/ 57, 104, 118 © Igorij/ 69 © Ivaylo Ivanov/ 19 © Jiang Hongyan/ 98 © Anna Hoychuk/ 14 © Ruslan Ivantsov/ 19 © Regina Jershova/ 8, 117, 146, 191 © Iakov Kalinin/ 21, 36 © Khram/ 5 © KhrobostovA/ 18, 77 © Kiboka/ 180 © Kontur-vid/ 14 © Volodymyr Krasyuk/ 2, 114 © Anna Kucherova/ 9, 248 © Kynata/ 194 © Elena Larina/ 79 © Leftleg/ 45 © Lepas/ 21, 46 © Gianna M/ 103, 204 © Madlen/ 74 © Iain McGillivray/ 85 © Viktar Malyshchyts/ 27 © Matin/ 8 © Maugli/ 228 © Dudarev Mikhail/ 128 © Beneda Miroslav/ 106, 109, 113, 233 © Molodec/ 182 © Gudrun Muenz/ 160 © Lisovskaya Natalia/ 98, 107, 149 © Nikiparonak/ 14 © Noraluca013/ 236 © Zhukov Oleg/ 226 © M. Unal Ozmen/ 52 © Pashabo/ 112 © Phloen/ 18, 127 © Picsfive/ 56 © Irina_QQQ/ 55 © Ravl/ 27, 44, 56, 73, 114, 118, 190, 206 © RetroClipArt/ 19 , 172 © Ryby/ 169 © Saiko3p/ 32 © Sarsmis/ 9, 16, 35, 57, 72, 76, 106, 119, 165, 188, 191, 192, 221 © Elena Schweitzer/ 8, 13 © Serg64/ 58 © Galayko Sergey/ 145 © Shebeko/ 200 © Serhiy Shullye/ 11, 25, 159 © Shutterstock/ 79 © Angel Simon/ 50 © Sinelyov/ 107 © Skyline/ 60 © B.G. Smith/ 196 © Danny Smythe/ 166 © Spaxiax/ 235 © Tanais/ 4, 76, 97, 187, 229 © Okhitina Tatyana/ 162, 231 © Andris Tkacenko/ 219 © Valentyn Volkov/ 120 © Vaaka/ 97, 154 © Kulish Viktoriia 91 © Dani Vincek/ cover, 72, 83, 89 © Marilyn Volan/ 86, 88, 139 © Volosina/ 73, 233 © Sandra Voogt/ 230 © Matka_Wariatka/ 26, 30, 214 ©Yasonya/ cover, multiple pages, abstract grunge circle rubber stamp, © Naci Yavuz/ 66, 88 © Peter Zijlstra.

By **Clipart ETC** © 2012 University of South Florida on pages: 2, 3, 4, 5, 6, 24, 26, 27, 44, 45, 50, 56, 57, 73, 106, 107, 120, 121, 164, 190, 191, 199, 206, 207.

By **Dover Publications, Inc.** © Cover, star throughout the book, other illustrations on pages 22, 166.

Other titles in this cookbook series:

Cooking with All Things Trader Joe's
by Deana Gunn & Wona Miniati
ISBN 978-0-9799384-8-1

Cooking with Trader Joe's: Companion
by Deana Gunn & Wona Miniati
ISBN 978-0-9799384-9-8

Cooking with Trader Joe's: Dinner's Done!
by Deana Gunn & Wona Miniati
ISBN 978-0-9799384-3-6

Cooking with Trader Joe's: Pack A Lunch!
by Céline Cossou-Bordes
ISBN 978-0-9799384-5-0

Cooking with Trader Joe's: Skinny Dish!
by Jennifer K. Reilly, RD
ISBN 978-0-9799384-7-4

Available everywhere books are sold.
Please visit us at

CookTJ.com